2020 VISION

for the
Christian Church (Disciples of Christ)

2020 VISION

for the
Christian Church (Disciples of Christ)

RICHARD L. HAMM

CHALICE
PRESS
St. Louis, Missouri

Cover photograph: © D. Jeanene Tiner
Cover design: Michael Domínguez
Interior design: Elizabeth Wright
Art director: Michael Domínguez

This book is printed on acid-free, recycled paper.

Visit Chalice Press on the World Wide Web at
www.chalicepress.com

10 9 8 7 6 5 4 3 2 1   02 03 04 05 06

Library of Congress Cataloging–in–Publication Data

Hamm, Richard L. (Richard Lee), 1947–
    2020 vision for the Christian church (Disciples of Christ) / Richard L. Hamm.
        p.   cm.
    ISBN 0-8272-3637-9 (pbk. : alk, paper)
    1. Christian Church (Disciples of Christ)–Doctrines. I. Title: Twenty twenty vision for the Christian church (Disciples of Christ). II. Title.
BX7321.2 .H35 2001
286.6'3 – dc21   2001000782

Printed in the United States of America

This book is dedicated to
the memory of my father,
Harold E. Hamm

Contents

Preface

*Whither shall I go from thy Spirit. Or whither shall I
flee from thy presence? If I ascend to heaven, thou art
there! If I make my bed in Sheol, thou art there! If I
take the wings of the morning and dwell in the
uttermost parts of the sea, even there thy hand shall
lead me, and thy right hand shall hold me.*

Psalm 139:7–10 (RSV)

Here's a test: "Hey kids, what time is it?"

Most Disciples in the United States are old enough to be
tempted to answer, "It's Howdy Doody time!"[1] At least that's a
better answer than "It's 1950!"

The fact is, it will be 2020 before we know it, and this is a
moment of *kairos* for the mainline churches of Jesus Christ!

In this volume I hope to begin to paint a picture of what we
look like when we *are* a faithful and growing church. Part of my
job as general minister and president is to be present across the
life of our church. Thus, in my years of service in this role I have
visited, observed, and spoken in hundreds of our congregations
and have been in each of our regions many times. I have seen
congregations that are boldly and faithfully facing up to the new
era in which we live; I have seen some that are clueless as to
what has changed and what that might mean; and I have seen
some that are furtively *resisting* appropriate change. Through
this firsthand experience, and through prayer and biblical and
theological reflection upon what I have seen, I believe I have
learned some things about us that are important for me to share.

I suppose some readers will be interested only in
congregations, believing that denominations are obsolete, soon

---

[1] The Howdy Doody Show was a national children's television program in the
early 1950s. At the beginning of each program, the host, "Buffalo Bob" Smith, would
ask, "Hey kids, what time is it?" The children present in the studio (sitting in what was
called the "peanut gallery") would shout in response, "It's Howdy Doody Time!"

ix

to be tossed onto the junk heap of history; however, every one of our congregations has been, and is, deeply impacted by the denomination of which it is a part. Of course, few today (thanks be to God) would make the argument that one's salvation depends on one's denominational affiliation, and the purposes of denominations are very different today than they were in the nineteenth century when our Disciples forebears rebelled against denominational*ism.* Nevertheless, denominations do continue to have an essential role that congregations ignore or dismiss at their own peril. I have addressed this matter at some length in appendix 1, and, if you believe denomination is irrelevant, you may wish to read that Appendix before proceeding to chapter 1. Likewise, if you do not have a working knowledge of how our church is governed (its polity), you may wish to read appendix 2 before proceeding.

As always, what I have written here is intended as an invitation to conversation with me and with one another. If we will but openly enter the dialogue, I believe we will together discern where God is leading us as congregations and as a whole church.

One thing we can know for certain: Some *change* is required of us as congregations and as a whole church if we are going to be faithful and growing in the years ahead. At a profound level, change is frightening to each of us. But John says, "Perfect love casts out fear...and whoever fears has not reached perfection in love" (1 Jn. 4:18b). Thus, our fear can be overcome, even our fear of change, and we can move forward into God's future for this church if we believe in the love of God made known in Jesus Christ. Thanks be to God!

"Whither shall I go from thy Spirit. Or whither shall I flee from thy presence?" asked the psalmist. There is nowhere we can go where God's presence is not with us—not even into the twenty-first century!

Acknowledgments

A number of people contributed greatly to the manuscript by reading it and making suggestions. I confess that I did not implement every suggestion, so any inadequacies in this book are mine, not theirs: Lori Adams, Charles Blaisdell, John Foulkes, Tom Jewell, Stan Litke, Don Manworren, Dan Moseley, Gay Reese, Richard Roland, Jack Sullivan, and Robert Welsh.

Much information was provided by Mike Naylor, Director of Research, and Larry Steinmetz, Editor of the Yearbook. Special assistance was provided by Curt Miller, Executive Director of the Office of Communication, and Cathy Hinkle of the Office of Communication.

The staff of the Office of the General Minister and President have all been supportive and helpful along the way, and I give thanks to God for these partners in ministry: Lori Adams, Sharon Coleman, Mary Collins, Bill Edwards, John Foulkes, Don Manworren, Curt Miller, Lois Artis Murray, Michael Naylor, Doris Speaks, Larry Steinmetz, and Jessica Vazquez.

I am indebted to Russ White, President of Christian Board of Publication, and David Polk, Editor of Chalice Press, who encouraged me and believed in the project even when I got woefully behind schedule.

As always, I must thank Mindy and dear friends who saw so many hours, days off, and holidays devoted to this project.

All biblical quotations are from the *New Revised Standard Version* unless otherwise noted.

CHAPTER 1

Our Context

For those who want to save their life will lose it, and
those who lose their life for my sake will find it.

Matthew 16:25

How can the Christian Church (Disciples of Christ) become
a more faithful and growing church in the years ahead?

This is the question that every one of our four thousand
congregations, thirty-five regions, eleven general units, and related
organizations and institutions must ask clearly and honestly in
order for us to move into the future God has for us as a church.

For this church, and all mainline churches, the past thirty
years have been traumatic. We have seen declines in membership
and in contributions for mission beyond the congregation. We
have gone through a period of blame and self-doubt, wondering
if there is some fatal flaw in the "Disciples way."

What we have discovered in recent years, however, is *not*
that our historical core values are somehow flawed. Nor has the
primary problem been the quality of our leadership. Rather,
there have been a number of other significant reasons for our
decline in size and strength. I will name just three.

First, there has been a huge shift in American culture. In my book *From Mainline to Front Line*,[1] I offered a brief analysis of how the world in general, and North American culture specifically, has changed drastically in the past fifty years. Sociologists and historians often mark 1968 as the year in which the disintegration of American mainline culture was sealed. It has taken most of the years since for mainline churches, including the Christian Church (Disciples of Christ), to begin to understand the sweeping implications of this massive shift of culture for the way we "do" church. In fact, many of our congregations and related institutions remain firmly rooted in the 1950s. Some of these simply do not yet understand the meaning of the incredible change that has occurred in the world. Others *mis*-understand the meaning of it and thus do not know how to respond to it. Still others understand it but hate the implications and resist them tooth and nail!

Positively stated, being a mainline church means that, since our inception, Disciples have had a significant role in shaping American culture. We did this largely through the great number of our members who are teachers in primary, secondary, and higher education and through the many schools we established through the years. We have also had our share of politicians (like Presidents James Garfield and Lyndon B. Johnson) and businesspeople (like J. Irwin Miller, the remarkable retired CEO of Cummins Diesel Corporation, who reads his New Testament in Greek and who sought to bring justice to the workplace and to the corporate boardroom).

Negatively stated, being a mainline church has meant that we have been overly dependent on "mainline" American culture to convey the concepts and language of our faith. Consequently, most of us have forgotten how to tell our faith story. It seems many of us have come to believe that our mission is merely to *keep the church doors open* so that anyone who wishes can meet us there. But these days, very few people wish to meet us there!

The seismic shift in American culture means, in part, that while it used to be assumed in most of this country that you were a Christian unless you said you weren't, now it is assumed

---

[1]Richard L. Hamm, *From Mainline to Front Line* (Lexington, Ky.: Lexington Theological Quarterly, 1996).

that you are *not* a Christian unless you say you *are*! In the minds of most Americans, especially those born after 1965, the church has gone from being a desirable place to find meaning and purpose to a place that is mostly unknown and assumed to be mostly irrelevant.

Although this cultural shift began in large measure in the 1960s and 1970s, we Disciples and the other mainline churches did not begin to understand what was happening until the 1990s. This is partly because even sociologists were having a hard time sorting out what was happening in our rapidly changing culture.

A second reason for the decline in our strength has been the fact that in the mid-1960s we nearly stopped establishing new Disciples congregations. Congregations have life cycles, just like people. Some live for centuries; others are rather short lived. For most of our nearly two-hundred-year history, we started more congregations than were dying. But from 1965 to 1980 we started almost no congregations at all. Finally, in the decade of the 1980s, we began to get serious about new congregation establishment again and set a goal of one hundred new congregations, ten per year for each of ten years. We reached our goal under the capable leadership of Jim Powell, who was then the executive director of the new church effort. But more than ten Disciples congregations die each year, and several more leave the denomination each year (which is sometimes a prelude to death as they cut themselves loose from their Disciples life support system).

Between 1980 and 2000, 237 Disciples congregations were started. During the same period, 534 congregations closed and 357 withdrew or were removed from the Yearbook because they did not report for ten years or more.

Do the math. Based on these numbers, an average of forty-five congregations die or otherwise depart each year. If we are going to grow, new congregation establishment will have to be an important part of our evangelism strategy.

A third reason for the decline of our strength has been our natural tendency, in the face of declining numbers, to become focused on institutional survival rather than on the true mission of the church. Jesus said, "Those who want to save their life will lose it." This is as true for institutions, including congregations and denominations, as it is for individuals. A passion for institutional survival soon begets an inward focus, an institutional rigidity, and a fear of change that is very unattractive to people who might otherwise be prospects for membership.

My favorite illustration of this phenomenon is the story of a certain town that was located along a river. The town built a bridge at some expense to make it possible for people to pass over the river. In order to recoup the cost of the bridge, they hired a person to be a toll collector. The money began coming in at a rapid pace. In fact, the town leaders decided they had better hire a bookkeeper to be certain that the funds were handled properly. But then they began to worry about security, so they hired a guard to protect the operation. Because they now had three employees, they decided they had better hire a manager, and then a human resources director. Predictably, the tolls began to fall somewhat short of the overhead. So a town meeting was called—and it was decided to fire the toll taker!

Our concern in the face of declining membership and money, our fear of death as an institution, has often driven us, in congregations and in other manifestations of the church, to do exactly the wrong things. Thus, we have created self-fulfilling prophecies, paralyzed in the face of a culture we no longer understand and a future about which we have no clue. (Note that being focused on institutional survival is not the same thing as focusing on institutional growth for the sake of mission!)

In the face of all this, Disciples church leaders have been seeking new clarity and vision in recent years. One of the most important fruits of this quest has been the Mission Imperative Statement, which reads as follows:

The Mission Imperative of the Christian Church (Disciples Of Christ)

In our quest to embody Christian unity, led and empowered by the Holy Spirit, we believe God calls us:

Our Vision

To be a faithful, growing church that demonstrates true community, deep Christian spirituality, and passion for justice. (Micah 6:8)

Our Mission

To be and to share the Good News of Jesus Christ, witnessing, loving, and serving from our doorsteps "to the ends of the earth." (Acts 1:8)

Our Imperative

To strengthen congregational life for this mission. (Ephesians 4:11–13, 15–16)

To accomplish this, we shall:

- Become the Good News
     Nurturing faith
     Practicing and teaching the spiritual disciplines
     Fostering Disciples identity
     Renewing congregational life
     Developing leaders

- Share the Good News
     Emphasizing ministry with children, youth
          young adults, and families
     Doing evangelism
     Establishing new congregations
     Creating ministries with older adults

- Serve from "our doorsteps to the ends of the Earth"
     Engaging in ministries of reconciliation,
          compassion, unity, and justice

In accepting our Vision, Mission, and Imperative, we affirm our need to:

- be an anti-racist/pro-reconciliation church
- strengthen relationships among all manifestations of the church
- share mutually and more fully the stewardship of God's gifts of our life in Christ
- encourage the growing diversity within our church family and community
- work with our many ecumenical and global partners to heal the brokenness of the body of Christ and human community

Approved by General Board Action: July 24, 2000

This document was created by the General Board to serve as a clarification of our mission, a clarification of what God is calling us to be and to do *today.*[2]

"Our mission: to be and to share the good news of Jesus Christ, witnessing and serving from our doorsteps to the ends of the earth." I think this is an excellent description of our mission. Let us note that the word *survival* does not appear in this statement!

The next most important sentence in the Mission imperative Statement is: *"...Our imperative: to strengthen congregational life for this mission."*

Our first mission field was the North American frontier, and we followed the Western migration, establishing congregations all along the way. As the old Disciples filmstrip "People of the Parentheses" put it, we were growing "like a raging prairie fire." But by 1890 the frontier was settled, so we turned our attention toward our second mission field, people overseas. And we were incredibly effective in many parts of the world. For example, the numbers of Disciples of Christ in the Democratic Republic of Congo today rival the numbers of Disciples in North America, and the church in Puerto Rico has grown by leaps and bounds.

Overseas ministries remain very important for a host of reasons, of course. But in the face of the cultural shift in the United States and Canada toward secularism, our primary mission field has once again become North America. We must no longer think of our congregations as "parishes." *Parish* is a word that comes from those European nations in which there was one state-supported church. A nation was divided into geographical areas called *"parishes,"* just as counties in Louisiana are called "parishes" today. Each parish had a church to which all those within the parish belonged. It was automatic. If you lived in the parish, you were enrolled in that parish church. It was *assumed* that everyone belonged to the church.

That was there and then. Here and now, our congregations are anything *but* parish churches to which people automatically come to be enrolled. Today, Disciples congregations must come to understand themselves as *mission stations.*

---

[2]The General Board is composed of 225 church leaders from all across North America. I believe the General Board is able to bring much wisdom to our quest for clarity and vision because it is composed mostly of members and leaders of congregations.

If you were going to evangelize in a foreign land, what is the first thing you would do? I think you would learn the language and learn everything you could about the people you were hoping to reach.

It is no different in our North American mission stations. We must learn everything we can about the people we are seeking to reach—their languages, their worldviews, their spiritual needs. We know a lot about the World War II generation and the Baby Boomer generation, but most of us know precious little about the younger generations who live in our mission field, that is, those born after 1965.

When we talk about understanding younger generations and understanding North American culture today, there are those who will rightly express the concern that we must not simply reshape ourselves to the culture's norms and standards. Of course not! As someone has said, "When you build a road *out* of Jerusalem, you are also building a road *into* Jerusalem!" But neither can we simply hang out in Jerusalem, safe behind its walls, tending its gates so as to allow entrance only to those whom we like, or only to those who reinforce what we always thought was true! If we are to be truly evangelical as a church, we cannot simply wait for people to meet us where we are. We must go out and meet people where *they* are.

I believe the Mission Imperative Statement is right on target. Another important piece of work done recently by the General Board was the identification of six vital issues. I believe these six vital issues are also right on target.

1. *Spiritual vitality and faith development.* Surely this *is* the first and most important issue. We cannot be and remain faithful to our mission apart from the spiritual disciplines.
2. *Leadership development.* How can we get anywhere without well-motivated and well-trained leadership, both clergy and lay?
3. *Congregational hospitality, diversity, and inclusiveness.* This speaks straight to the world we see emerging all around us.
4. *Ministries of evangelism and witness.* This can no longer mean simply inviting people with no church to our church. This now means bringing people of *no* faith *to* faith. This

means personal evangelism, and it means establishing new congregations.

5. *Strong worship life.* How can we be sustained for the journey, how can we sing the Lord's song in this strange new land, unless we share a strong worship life that keeps us focused on who it is that calls us and sustains us?

6. *Ministries of justice, reconciliation, service, and public advocacy.* These are essential ways in which we express our faith and participate in what God is seeking to do in the world.

These six vital issues are focal points for our transformation into the church God calls us to become—a church that is faithful and growing, that is living out its mission imperative, that manifests the vision of true community, a deep Christian spirituality, and a passion for justice.

But how do we get from here to there? How do we go from being a church that is, in some ways, a church of the 1950s to a faithful and growing church for the world that is becoming? I believe a helpful way to proceed is to think about what God may be calling us to be and to do in the year 2020. I like the idea of focusing on the year 2020 for a number of reasons.

First, we tend to be locked into one- or two-year views of the future because that is the typical length of our budget cycles. In each of our individual parts of this institution called the Christian Church (Disciples of Christ), we tend to think, *If only we can get through this budget period, then we'll see what's next.* That sort of short-term vision tends to make things that really aren't terribly important seem important and to make things that are really quite important seem unimportant. For example, seen from the short-term "survivalist" view, children and youth are not very important because they will not be financially contributing members for a long time. But taking the long-term view of twenty years or more, we recognize in our children and youth the future leadership and core of the church. A twenty-year visioning process helps lift our eyes above the usual one- or two-year horizon, yet does not look so far forward as to lose all focus and concreteness.

Second, I like the idea of focusing on the year 2020 because it does organize our work on the vital issues around a particular time, which will help us structure our work as we think about how to get from here to there.

Third, twenty years constitutes a generation. Although we often say, "The church is always only one generation from destruction," focusing on the year 2020 challenges us to see ourselves as only one generation from reformation and revitalization.

Fourth, lots of Disciples who are grandparents want a church for their grandchildren, and they know that the present Christian Church (Disciples of Christ) is mostly not it. They can get excited about helping this become a church for the next generation.

Fifth, the demographics of North America in the year 2020 will make this an even more multicultural, multiracial mission field. If we are going to be anything other than a predominantly white church in 2020, we must become intentional now about becoming a church for 2020. This gives real urgency to our intention to become an antiracist/pro-reconciliation church.

Finally, I like focusing on the year 2020 because it presses us to take children, youth, and young adults seriously. If we continue to focus on attracting mostly Baby Boomers, in twenty years most of our congregations will look just like most of them look now—old![3]

It is tempting to seek to bring transformation to the church (congregationally, regionally, and generally) through mere structural change alone. Goodness knows we have need for structural change! Most congregations were organized or reorganized in the 1940s and 1950s for an era that ended in 1968. As a denomination, we organized ourselves in 1968 for an era that ended *in* 1968!

Of course, structural change is an ongoing, necessary process. But, in my years as general minister and president, I have found that trying to bring transformation through structural change mostly begets resistance and territorialism. Thus, we must begin with *mission and relationship*. That is, we must begin by *working together in ways that get the job done faithfully and effectively.* By approaching reformation and revitalization in this way, we can become energized by the creation of "covenantal partnerships"

---

[3]I feel I can say this because, in regard to Baby Boomers, I *are* one!

(what the corporate world calls "strategic alliances") around the vital issues.

Denominationally these covenantal partnerships will naturally cross over old bureaucratic and manifestational lines. *Congregationally* these partnerships will naturally move us away from the old "functional committee system." As we find these new faithful and effective ways of working together, structures will naturally begin to change to follow relationships.

So I invite you to begin thinking in terms of 2020, both for your congregation and for this communion called the Christian Church (Disciples of Christ). I invite you to begin the process of developing 2020 vision, of becoming the church God is calling us to be, by thinking about what 2020 will be like as best we can see it and how we can work together to fulfill our calling "to be and to share the good news of Jesus Christ, witnessing and serving from our doorsteps to the ends of the earth."

I believe this is an exciting journey that lies ahead, a journey toward a new faithfulness and growth for the Christian Church (Disciples of Christ). I am grateful to be on the journey with you!

Questions for Reflection and Discussion

1. In what ways does your congregation function like a "parish"?
2. In what ways does your congregation function like a "mission station"?
3. In what ways do you think your congregation could function more like a mission station?
4. Which of the six vital issues are being addressed most effectively in your congregation?
5. Which of the six are being addressed least effectively?

CHAPTER 2

A Call To Integrity and Transformation

*In Christ God was reconciling the world to himself, not
counting their trespasses against them, and entrusting
the message of reconciliation to us. So we are
ambassadors for Christ, since God is making his
appeal through us.*

2 Corinthians 5:19–20

Most of us know the Christmas story by heart, but it suddenly
had a new impact on me when I visited Bethlehem for the first
time in 1985. I had seen a number of important sites in Jerusalem
earlier in the day, including the Mount of Olives. These were
very moving. Still, I was unprepared for the experience I was
about to have in Bethlehem.

When people visit the Holy Land, they become obsessed
with "walking in the footsteps of Jesus and Paul." No matter how
cynical you may be when your official guide tells you with
certainty, "This is the actual spot where such and such happened"
(when you know that no one knows for sure about the exact
location of many of the sites), still you become obsessed with

walking in the footsteps of Jesus and Paul. You find yourself thinking, *Wow, Jesus was actually here in this place!* It is a powerful experience as you find yourself suddenly standing inside those stories you learned in Sunday school.

As with most traditional locations of significant biblical events, there is a church standing over the traditional site of Jesus' birth. Modern-day crèche scenes to the contrary, the stable of Bethlehem was likely a limestone cave, since that area is so full of such caves, which provided convenient shelter for animals.

Inside the Church of the Nativity, our guide led us down steps that took us under the altar to a plain cave that has been venerated since at least the second century as the birthplace of Jesus. In this small candlelit cave the guide had the seven of us stand in a circle and sing "Silent Night." Now, as schmaltzy as this may sound to some, I have to tell you that I had a feeling come over me such as I had never before experienced. It was only a few minutes before we were back in the tour bus and on our way to another site, but for the next several hours, every few minutes the thought would pop into my head, *Wow, right here in Bethlehem was the place where God chose to be revealed to the world in the person of Jesus the Christ!* Every time this thought popped into my head I found my eyes welling up with tears of wonder and joy.

There was something about being in Bethlehem. It was not about that particular cave, which may or may not be the actual site. But the biblical witness is clear that it was in this small burg of Bethlehem that Jesus was born. Being in Bethlehem was like standing in a doorway through which God had come into the world in a powerful incarnate way. It gave a concrete quality to the story that I had never before experienced in quite the same way.

I have thought about that experience many times in the years since. I came to realize that 2 Corinthians 5:17–20 really captures the quintessential import of the story. Paul says in verse 19, "In Christ God was reconciling the world to himself, not counting their trespasses against them, and entrusting the message of reconciliation to us." This is the faith of the apostles in a nutshell: "In Christ God was reconciling the world to himself, not counting their trespasses against them." It is so straightforward that even a simple person can grasp it. Yet it is so profound that theologians and mystics can spend a lifetime plumbing its depths. The story of redemption is like a multifaceted gem.

"In Christ God Was Reconciling the World to Himself..."

So much of religion is about trying to get God to accept us, to get God to do what we want God to do. But the Christian faith turns that kind of religion right on its head! We do not have to get God to accept us. God *does* accept us and loves us just as we are. It is when we realize this truth that we are really *transformed* from people who are merely trying to do what is not against the Law of God to people who are seeking to do what will bring God joy because we love God.

We do not have to try to get God's attention. "Hey, God! I am here! Do you see me? I am so sorry for my sins. Is there anything I could possibly do to be reconciled with you?"

The amazing thing about this story is that God took the initiative! God was in Christ, "reconciling the world to Himself." God did not wait for humankind to come around, *God took the initiative!* The God whom we know in Jesus Christ is not simply some disinterested Spirit who created the world and then retired to some far corner of the universe. This God is a God who wants relationship with us, who cares about what is happening in our personal everyday lives and in our world. This is a God who reaches out to *us*! As John says, "For God so *loved* the world that he gave his only Son." "We love because [God] first loved us."

"In Christ God was reconciling the world to himself."

"...Not Counting Their Trespasses against Them"

So much of common religion is about score keeping. In this sort of religion, God is a sort of Gilbert and Sullivan character who's "got a little list." On that list are the good things we do and the bad things we do, and in the end its a matter of which outweighs the other. Well, that may be great Persian Zoroastrianism, or it might be good Babylonian theology, but it is not Christian faith.

I will never forget the Sunday one of the elders of a congregation I served (which shall go unnamed) stood at the table and concluded his communion prayer by saying, "Lord, forgive us our sins and restore us to a right relationship with you—provided we are worthy." I wanted to shout, "Good grief! That's not the gospel of Jesus Christ! That's the culture's version of the gospel, which is not good news at all! In fact, it's bad news!" I restrained myself from shouting (I guess I have learned *something* about ministry), but I resolved then and there to do some teaching with our elders.

We do not get God's love because we are worthy or because we have somehow *earned* it. As Paul says in Romans (5:7–8), "Rarely will anyone die for a righteous person—though perhaps for a good person someone might actually dare to die. But God proves his love for us in that while we still were sinners Christ died for us."

"Amazing grace, how sweet the sound that saved a wretch like me." I know, a lot of us do not like to be called wretches, and yet, I have to admit that apart from the love of Jesus Christ I can be pretty wretched. But God did not wait for us to get over our wretchedness before reaching out to us. "In Christ God was reconciling the world to himself, not counting their trespasses against them."

"…And Entrusting the Message of Reconciliation to Us"

Think about this. *We* are entrusted with the message of reconciliation. God believes in us. We are usually preoccupied with the question "Do we believe in God?" But the fact is that God believes in us! Why else would God entrust to *us* the message of reconciliation?

There is an oft-told story in which an angel is speaking to Jesus in heaven after his ascension. The angel inquires about what the next steps are in Jesus' plan for the salvation of humankind. Jesus explains that he has left behind a number of disciples to spread the good news. The angel says, "Well, if that does not work, what is your backup plan?" Jesus answers, "I have no other plan."

"So," as Paul says, "we are ambassadors for Christ, since God is making his appeal through us." What a magnificent calling, what a responsibility—to share the good news of salvation in Jesus Christ!

In the Old Testament book of Judges, we find that a good judge might rule Israel for forty years or more. During that time, the nation would typically obey the law and honor the covenant. But in the years when an ineffective judge ruled, no one would tell the story of Israel's sojourn in Egypt and how God redeemed them and brought them into the promised land. Soon the people would forget about Yahweh and the covenant. So for several hundred years Israel went through successive periods in which the people would remember the covenant and prosper for a time, and then forget the covenant and fall into hard times and foreign domination. From one generation to the next, the people could actually forget their story and thus forget Yahweh and the covenant.

It is true that the church is always just one generation from destruction. Unless we tell the story to each succeeding generation, the story is forgotten and the church dies.

Jesus has no other plan! It is up to us to share the story of redemption. *"We are ambassadors for Christ, since God is making his appeal through us."*

In the words of H. Ernest Nichol's hymn:

We've a story to tell to the nations
[including the United States and Canada]
that shall turn their heart to the right,
a story of truth and mercy,
a story of peace and light.

We've a song to be sung to the nations
that shall lift their hearts to the Lord;
a song that shall conquer evil
and shatter the spear and sword.

This is the story that called the church of Jesus Christ into being, and it is the story the church of Jesus Christ is called to tell.

As we think about the revitalization of our congregations and of our whole denomination, we sometimes try to begin someplace other than the gospel story. For example, we look to management science and the latest theories of organizational life and change. We look to marketing for better ways to get our church before the public. Such resources as these are not bad.

On the contrary, we need all the management science and marketing savvy we can get. But the employment of these insights is not the core of revitalization. The core of revitalization is recommitment to the gospel of Jesus Christ, the story of redemption: *"In Christ God was reconciling the world to himself, not counting their trespasses against them, and entrusting the message of reconciliation to us. So we are ambassadors for Christ, since God is making his appeal through us."*

Understanding and committing to this, the "apostolic faith," the "old, old story," is the core issue of revitalization, the core issue for being a faithful and growing church in the years ahead. Although the mediums of music, the forms of worship, and the approaches to organizational life employed by the church will change from time to time as they have in the past, the basic spiritual needs of all humanity do not change. While the ways by which we tell the story change from generation to generation, and while our understanding of the implications of the story for our day-to-day life and behavior may change as we and the church more fully understand the story's meaning, the story itself remains the same. It is out of this good news of Jesus Christ that the values and vision that give the church life and vitality flow.

If we, as the Christian Church (Disciples of Christ), are going to be effective ambassadors for Christ, we have to get the story straight and we have to go beyond *telling* the story. We must *live* the story, we must *live* the faith, *with integrity*. We must live the faith with integrity as individuals, surely. But the institutional life of our church must also exhibit this integrity and congruence with the story.

Yet, as we all know, there is a tendency for the day-to-day life of the individual Christian to become separated from the Christian values and vision that give purpose to that individual's life. We share this malady with no less a person than the apostle Paul, who said, "So I find it to be a law that when I want to do what is good, evil lies close at hand. For I delight in the law of God in my inmost self, but I see in my members another law at war with the law of my mind, making me captive to the law of sin that dwells in my members. Wretched man that I am!" (Rom. 7:21–24).

In the same way, there is a tendency for the day-to-day life and operation of an institution to become separated from the values and vision that give that institution purpose. This separation of *means* from *ends* creates institutions that are ineffective and even counterproductive.

One thinks, for example, of a government welfare office, the vision and values of which have to do with lifting people out of poverty and into self-reliance. However, welfare institutions have a tendency to slip into an attitude that treats their clients as "numbers" rather than as persons, and so clients end up feeling discouraged and dehumanized instead of helped and uplifted. Thus, the cycle of poverty is reinforced by one of the very institutions that is supposed to help break it.

Another example is in the retail industry. We have all encountered retail stores whose avowed purpose is to serve customers, but whose actual day-to-day practice has become that of serving its own employees.

This tendency for the day-to-day life and operation of an institution to become separated from the values and vision that give it purpose is as real in the institutions of the church as in any other institution. This means, in part, that the church must constantly work to keep its day-to-day institutional life and operation connected with the Christian values and vision that inspire its essential nature and character.

Jesus Christ came to create a ministry that sought to reconnect God's values, vision, and *intentions* for life on earth with the everyday *realities* of life on earth. He came challenging the people and the institutions of his day to live according to God's intentions for them. But the world resisted this reconnection, to the point of crucifying the Christ. The church, which the New Testament calls the *body of Christ*, is called to be the same kind of incarnation (embodiment) of the Divine on earth as was Christ himself. That is, the church is called to incarnate or embody God's vision and values for humankind. Another way to say this is that God has called the church to both *be* and *do* the gospel of Jesus Christ. The book of Acts is the story of the early disciples' efforts to incarnate (embody) faithfully the values and vision Christ revealed in that new institution called "the church."

Those times in history when the church has failed utterly to embody these divine values are when *leadership* has failed to connect those divine values and the divine vision that they espouse with the day-to-day operation of the institution. Such duplicitous leadership is often unconscious, a product of being too immersed in the surrounding culture of pragmatism and "success." When it is conscious, it is often justified with phrases such as "We must be realistic" and "By compromising now, it will be possible for us to accomplish our larger purposes later." Nevertheless, the end results of such compromise usually look like the means employed to achieve them and are usually less than that for which we had hoped.

Of course, it is not easy to hold together our values and vision with our day-to-day life, individually or institutionally. Thus, we have to struggle with holding the two together the best we can, making our ends and means as congruent as possible, trusting the grace of God in our failures.

It is an important struggle. If we simply allow our means and ends to become separated, choosing our means without reference to God's values and vision for the church, we will not incarnate anything that has the substance of Christ. Therefore, as an institution, our church must seek to live day-to-day in a way that corresponds to that which the church is called to become. We must be in a constant state of spiritual and institutional renewal, because the world is very powerful in its ability to lure and entice us (Jas. 1:14) into means that are not consistent with the ends we are called to seek.

Just as we must struggle to hold together means and ends, so we must resist the temptation to separate spiritual renewal and institutional renewal. These must not be separate "compartments" of church life, or else we have again fallen into the trap of separating means from ends. In spite of a sincere desire for real renewal, we could nevertheless find ourselves merely restructuring without addressing our spiritual need. Or we could find ourselves merely seeking spiritual renewal without seeking to embody that renewal in our structures.

Peter Morgan[1] likes to speak of the spiritual and institutional aspects of the church as electricity and wire. Indeed, all the

---

[1] President of the Disciples of Christ Historical Society.

electricity in the world will not do much if there are no means by which to conduct it. But all the wire in the world will not do much if there is no electricity to conduct. Thus, we cannot simply focus on increasing the voltage and amperage of our spiritual life, nor can we focus simply on the gauge and condition of our institutional/structural forms. We must seek at once to be both truly renewed spiritually and truly an incarnation or embodiment of that renewed spirit.

In fact, I believe even "renewal" falls short of that to which God is calling us as the church of Jesus Christ. I believe God is calling us to be nothing less than *transformed.* Transformation comes as we seek renewal and as we open ourselves to the power of God. Through this synergy of our effort and God's action through the Holy Spirit, our spiritual and institutional life begins to merge into one incarnated whole.

To take our electrical metaphor a bit further, more than conduction takes place when electricity flows through wire; fields of energy are generated across the electromagnetic spectrum. Heat is generated, radio waves are generated, and, under the right conditions, light is generated! Electric companies place a "transformer" on a service pole to "transform" the electrical current in the high voltage lines into a power that can be used throughout the neighborhood. The church needs both to become transformed and to become a transformer, so that we can both have the divine power we need and so that we can apply that power to daily life in appropriate and effective ways. This is expressed in the diagram on the next page.

Of course, such transformation is not a once-and-for-all event. It comes and goes in greater and lesser degrees. Transformation is a way of life in which we daily offer up our best efforts to God, and the Holy Spirit transforms these gifts into faithful incarnations of Christ. As North American Disciples, given to pragmatic approaches and to "doing it ourselves," we can easily leave the Holy Spirit out of it. Without the Holy Spirit, we may achieve *some* institutional renewal and perhaps even a kind of spiritual renewal, but we will never experience real transformation into a faithful incarnation.

My hope in this book, then, is to begin to address the vision God has for this church and its institutional realities in a way that seeks to bring them together and hold them together in a faithful incarnation.

Figure 2-1

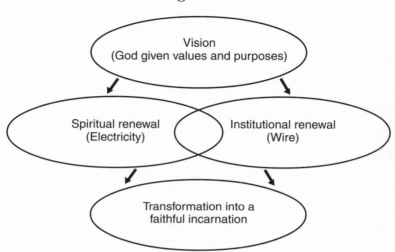

I could have written only about the vision God holds before the church (a part of spiritual renewal). Or I could have written only about our institutional challenges. But what I hope to accomplish here is some bringing together of these two forms of renewal, thus helping the church move toward being transformed by the Holy Spirit into a faithful incarnation of that which God has called us to be and to share: the good news of Jesus Christ.

Questions for Reflection and Discussion

1. As you think about your own faith, do you seem to focus primarily on "trying not to do what is against the Law of God" or do you primarily seek "to do what will bring God joy" because you love God?
2. In what ways do you live the faith with integrity? In what ways do you not?
3. In what ways does your congregation live the faith with integrity? In what ways not?
4. What is the current health of your congregation's spiritual dimensions (the electricity)?
5. What is the current health of your congregation's institutional dimensions (the wire)?

PART I

The Vision

To be a faithful, growing church that manifests

- true community

- a deep Christian spirituality

- a passion for justice

Introduction

James Russell Lowell's great hymn says, "New occasions teach new duties."[1] We are living in the midst of a very new occasion, and it is incumbent upon us to discern what new duties represent faithfulness in this generation, what new things God is seeking to do among us. As general minister and president in this time of the turning of the centuries and the millennia, I see my role as helping the church come together around the right questions. I do not regard myself as an "answer man," although I do have some ideas and suggestions. But my *primary* role is to bring the church together around the right *questions.* Together we Disciples, in consultation with our ecumenical partners, have enough brain power and enough spiritual power to discern what God would have us do and be in this new day.

The problem is not, of course, that God is hiding from us, or being coy, or otherwise trying to make it difficult for us to receive a vision of what we Disciples are to be and to do. The problem is that in the midst of the incredibly rapid pace of change that has been going on all around us the past thirty years or so, we have become overwhelmed and often confused. In our bewilderment, many of us have gone years without practicing the spiritual disciplines, and thus we have often been ill prepared to receive the visions God has for us.

I first laid out what I regard as a vision for this church at the Pittsburgh General Assembly in 1995. I called it "Three Marks of a Faithful Church." Whatever work we feel called to do, I believe there are three marks—indeed, three *benchmarks*—that must inform and shape all our efforts to become a fruitful church in today's world.

As I have named them, the three marks of a faithful church are (1) true community, (2) a deep Christian spirituality, and (3) a passion for justice. I did not dream these up! They come straight out of the prophet Micah. He said, "Do justice...love

---

[1] James Russell Lowell, "Once To Every Man and Nation," 1845.

kindness [that's true community]...and walk humbly with your God [that's spirituality]" (Mic. 6:8). In the New Testament (Mt. 23:23), Jesus describes "the weightier matters of the law: justice and mercy [community] and faith [spirituality]."

Although I did not simply dream up these "three marks of a faithful church," they do represent my own understanding and conviction of that toward which God is calling this church. I believe that whatever we discern together to be God's vision for us as a communion will certainly not contradict these three marks of a faithful church: true community, a deep Christian spirituality, and a passion for justice.

There are congregations among us that pride themselves on their community. They hug each other and stage marvelous fellowship dinners and field softball teams and offer aerobics classes. And yet some of them are lacking because they have little concern for those beyond their fellowship, and their worship services are empty of real encounter with the Holy Spirit. This is not true community!

There are congregations among us that pride themselves on what they consider to be their spirituality. They use religious language easily, they engage in very visible acts of piety, they have worship services that are perhaps best described as "productions." Yet in some of these congregations it all rings hollow because, far from manifesting true community, there are power struggles, and people are often treated badly; there is no detectable concern for justice or even for charity. This is not a deep Christian spirituality!

There are congregations among us who pride themselves on their outreach ministries of justice and compassion, and yet, in some of these congregations, they are hostile to one another, and their worship services seem empty of spiritual power. Some of their justice ministries are fruitless, but they seem not to care about effectiveness. It seems that it's not having a real impact on the world that matters so much to them as "being right on the issues." They don't have so much of a "passion for justice" as they do a "pride for justice." These folks are often frustrated, "burned out," and feeling angry and hopeless because they are cut off from the one thing that will keep them energized and fresh: true communion with the Holy Spirit and with one another.

My point here is that a church cannot choose one or two of these three marks and still be whole and healthy. A congregation (and a denomination, for that matter) must manifest all three marks to be whole, healthy, and vital.

Further, in order to manifest effectively the first and third marks (true community and a passion for justice), a congregation and denomination must be rooted in a deep Christian spirituality. It is only as there is real connection with God that either true community or a passion for justice can be sustained. Without a deep Christian spirituality we are trying to do community and justice simply on the strength of our own good intentions.

Thus, a spirituality that does not manifest itself in true community and a passion for justice is not authentically Christian. And in order for true community and a passion for justice to be sustained, they must be rooted in a deep Christian spirituality.

CHAPTER 3

True Community

I give you a new commandment, that you love one
another. Just as I have loved you, you also should love
one another. By this everyone will know that you are
my disciples, if you have love for one another.

John 13:34–35

Micah said that one of God's requirements is that we "love kindness." Jesus said it even more strongly on the night when he was betrayed, which we call Maundy Thursday. "Maundy" comes from the same root as the word "commandment," and it was on Maundy Thursday that Jesus gave us what he called in the passage above a "new commandment."

Later the same evening, as recorded in John 17:20–21, Jesus prayed that his disciples would be one so that the world would believe that he was truly sent by God.

This is nothing less than a call for the church to be a community—a *true* community. Jesus considered this to be one of the essential marks of his church. He knew that if the church manifested true community, the world would recognize Christ in them! As Jesus said (Lk. 17:21), "The kingdom is in the midst of you" (RSV), or, literally, "between you." The world in the time of Jesus' earthly ministry was a world where true community was hard to find—so rare that if people actually saw it they would recognize it, desire it, be led to it, and thereby be led to the Christ.

And what of today? If there ever was a generation that needed to see true community embodied, this is it! Our society is more accurately described as enclaves of entrepreneurialism than as community. In this era of individualism, personal isolation, and loneliness, so many people are so hungry for community; yet community is based in trust, and people today find it difficult to trust because they have learned that purely human community (which is based on mere goodwill) is not dependable.

What if there *were* a dependable, "true community" available? What if there were a community based not merely on people's being alike, or thinking alike, or merely liking each other, a community based not on the goodwill of its members, but a community that intentionally invited the living Christ to be at its center? What if there were a community that continually confessed its dependence upon God and that actively sought to be led by the Holy Spirit toward wholeness and health? Would not vast numbers of persons be drawn to such a community?

Jesus knew what he was asking for when he commanded us to love one another. Such community is perhaps the most powerful evangelistic force in the world.

But has the church of Jesus Christ been this kind of community? More to the point, is *our* own communion, the Christian Church (Disciples of Christ), this kind of community? Have we been obedient to Christ's new commandment to love one another?

Sometimes.

Why isn't the answer "always"? Well, the answer isn't "always" because nothing this side of the Realm of God is perfect, including the church.

But why isn't the answer even "usually"? Because the church has not made it a point to keep Christ at the center of its life. We have often tried to do church on the basis of good intentions, rather than on the basis of lives that have been submitted to Christ in obedience. *Our congregations tend to be social organizations rather than spiritual organisms.* Sometimes it's hard to tell the difference between a social club and a congregation. Clubs are organized to meet the common social goals of their members, not to be the embodiment of the living Christ, as the church is called to be.

The church is certainly divine, but it is also very human, and this is nowhere more apparent than in the way we sometimes treat each other in the church. The basic problem is that we who claim to be Christians are often much too willful; that is, we have sometimes not really surrendered ourselves (heart, soul, and mind) and allowed ourselves to be filled by the indwelling of the Holy Spirit. We sometimes remain in charge of ourselves, without really submitting to Christ. We don't *like* the language of submission, which is understandable in the face of how "submission" has usually been interpreted by the powerful to the powerless and the oppressed. But our congregations can never be *true communities* of faith until we individually and collectively submit to Christ and the Holy Spirit!

In Galatians 2:20, Paul says, "It is no longer I who live, but it is Christ who lives in me. And the life I now live in the flesh I live by faith in the Son of God, who loved me and gave himself for me." Everything the church is called by Christ to be assumes that this kind of experience marks the lives of most of the church's members, or *at least the lives of its leaders*!

I remember the story of an elder who was sitting in a board meeting one night while a discussion was going on about some matter of importance in that congregation. Someone said something that sparked his anger. As the conversation proceeded, he could feel his anger rising until he could stand it no more. He jumped to his feet, ready to tell them all what he thought about their "stupid idea." But just as he was about to open his mouth, he remembered something. He slowly sat down and mumbled, "I'm sorry, I almost forgot. Dead men don't speak." ("It is no longer I who live, but it is Christ who lives in me" [Gal. 2:20].)

The point here is not that we should never have an opinion or that we should never boldly tell the truth as we understand it. The point is, as Paul says, to "speak the truth in love," not in a way that lacks humility or that seeks to intimidate others. However, my twenty-two years of experience as a pastor of congregations leads me to believe that there is usually more going on in most congregational fights than a mere passion for truth. There is usually some seeking of power and control involved.

In contemporary society, many people feel powerless and victimized. Some of us will remember that galvanizing scene in the movie *Network,* in which the central character sticks his head out a window of his apartment and shouts to the world, "I'm mad as hell and I'm not gonna take it anymore!" It was an outpouring of angst with which most modern and postmodern North Americans can identify. In significant ways, our lives seem to be out of our control and in the control of invisible forces that are expressions of unbridled capitalism, bureaucracy, big politics, and uncontrollable change. People bring these feelings of powerlessness to church with them, and I believe it is in large measure this growing sense of powerlessness that has led to the growing incidence of power struggles and destructive conflict in congregations. Churches with a congregational polity, like the Christian Church (Disciples of Christ), are particularly vulnerable to these kinds of power struggles.[1] But it is not only in the congregation that we Disciples have to beware of power politics! It is found in all three manifestations. We Disciples "cut our teeth" on nineteenth-century American politics, and we are still "biting" one another regularly![2]

The Impact of the American Context on the Disciples

This church began on the American frontier in the earliest days of this nation. It was a time of rugged individualism. The ideas of John Locke, which in many ways shaped this nascent democracy, also shaped the Disciples of Christ. In fact, as I have studied the matter, I have been amazed at how intertwined the United States and the Stone-Campbell movement were in the nineteenth century. The Cane Ridge meeting occurred just twelve

---

[1] "Polity" refers to the type of organization or government of a church. A "congregational polity" is one in which the congregation retains the right to make all decisions in matters of the congregation's property, policy, the calling of ministers and other staff, and so forth.
[2] Although it is the historical connections to the United States that are treated here for the most part, Disciples in Canada trace their origins not only to the Stone-Campbell movement but also to Scottish Baptists, who were shaped by many of the same ideas and struggles.

years after the Constitution of the United States came into force. The theme of "America as the Promised Land through which God will bless the world in a special way" was very much a part of Alexander Campbell's worldview. In fact, he made sure that Bethany College commencement ceremonies were always held on July Fourth!

If you visit the Campbell home in Bethany, West Virginia, you will find a historical display on the second floor. As I was browsing through this display one day, I saw something I had not seen before. Next to a picture of Alexander Campbell standing in the Virginia Constitutional Convention was a display featuring the very first missionary sent out by the American Christian Missionary Society, James Barclay. I read there that, as a young man, Barclay purchased Monticello from Thomas Jefferson's family, refurbished it, and lived in it for a number of years! This is just one small example of how intertwined the Stone-Campbell movement has been with the history of the United States.

This intertwining of history between the young nation and this religious movement means that many attitudes and perspectives were held in common as well. The nation was born in rebellion against a king's authority that was exercised from afar for purposes that were not always in the interests of his colonial subjects. Likewise, the Disciples of Christ were born in rebellion against denominational authority that it was felt had been abused.[3]

We were a *movement* precisely because we embodied popular attitudes regarding authority. Chief among these attitudes was the belief that, apart from God,[4] the individual is the ultimate authority. This belief gave rise to a national constitution that is built on "checks and balances" designed to prevent the abuse of power by any branch or entity of government. This belief in individualism also gave rise to the Stone-Campbell religious movement, which was based on the autonomy of the individual and the congregation.

---

[3]In the case of Alexander Campbell, it was the power of the presbytery to decide who was and was not fit to take communion.

[4]In this case, *God* is a generic, deistic expression that refers more to the order of nature than to the personal God revealed in Jesus Christ.

Now, I believe the concept of "local and individual autonomy" as it has been lived out by Disciples has generally been a positive thing. It is an "engine" that has created a great deal of energy and ownership among our people. In fact, when "whole church" initiatives in the Christian Church (Disciples of Christ) have failed, it has usually been because of a failure to provide adequate time and processes by which to develop full ownership of such initiatives by our members. Those "whole church" initiatives that have succeeded have done so because people were invited to participate in the shaping of outcomes rather than simply "handed" a decision made elsewhere. Nevertheless, I believe we also have to confess that a polity rooted in autonomy easily begets sin. Literally, *autonomy* means "a law unto itself," which is a concept that is certainly foreign to the Realm of God. Whatever value autonomy has for us can be in regard only to the prevention of the abuse of authority as it relates to the human side of the church's governance. Taken to its extreme, a polity of individual and congregational autonomy makes it impossible for leaders to lead because those who are called to follow will never grant anyone the authority necessary to lead.

I believe it is fair to say that, until 1968, rather than our polity being based on an ecclesiology[5] that was informed by the American political system, our polity was based on American political philosophy and was only from time to time informed by a clear and purposeful ecclesiology!

Prior to 1968 we Disciples were simply an association of autonomous congregations, agencies, and institutions. We feared the tyranny of denominational judicatory as much as eighteenth-century Americans had resented the tyranny of a King George. In 1968 we finished a decade-long process called "restructure." Through this process, we expressed our desire to become a *church* rather than a mere association of autonomous congregations, agencies, and institutions. We changed our name, in fact, from the Christian *Churches* (Disciples of Christ) to the Christian *Church* (Disciples of Christ). In this "restructure" we attempted to move

---

[5]"Ecclesiology" refers to how a church is visibly organized in order to reflect its invisible spiritual nature. There is no single ecclesiology in the New Testament, so the various communions within the church universal have each sought to develop an ecclesiology that they believe is faithful and helpful.

our polity from a mostly political basis to a basis of "covenant," as is laid out in our principal document of governance, *The Design.*

A Call for Change in Our Church's Culture

But while restructure redistributed power in some ways, it did not effectively address the underlying problem of Disciples, which is our preoccupation with our own personal power and autonomy. We have never effectively addressed the fact that we have in this church a "culture of autonomy" that goes beyond healthy distrust of human power to the distrust of anything we cannot personally control.

In such a culture of autonomy, we are seldom willing to give anyone the authority to do anything on anyone's behalf, nor to represent anyone in any matter of importance. This problem is often manifested in our relationships with God as well.

In the face of this problem, I do not propose that we should throw out *The Design.* I do not think *The Design* is the problem, although it needs to be adjusted from time to time, as must any governance document. What I am calling for is an adjustment in our *attitude* and especially in the way we live within *The Design.* I am calling for a change in our church's culture, from a culture of autonomy to a culture of interdependence.

Early in my service as general minister and president, I thought what we needed was to move from a culture of autonomy to a culture of cooperation. But now I do not believe *cooperation* is radical enough. We really do need a culture of interdependence—a culture in which we really are depending on one another, a culture in which we are really trusting one another, a culture where we make real commitments to one another and are not always holding out the right to withdraw our support whenever we feel like it. Such a culture of interdependence is essential for true community. Please understand that I do not wish to attempt to *legislate* this kind of trust and mutual commitment. But I do wish for us to create the kinds of systems and structures that will nurture and support such a culture of interdependence. We presently have a number of systems, structures, and styles in all three manifestations that practically guarantee we will be in competition with each other, and we need to address these structural issues. But the primary problem, in my opinion, is our own attitudes, our own fierce and fearful determination not to submit to anybody or anything (often not even to God!).

Although we Stone-Campbell people pride ourselves on our restoration of New Testament forms, the kind of autonomy we Disciples have typically practiced is not really justifiable on the basis of the New Testament. Read Romans 12 and 1 Corinthians 12 again and remember that these are passages where Paul speaks of the church as a body with interdependent parts. No part of a living body can claim that it doesn't need the other parts. A *dead* body's parts can exist in total autonomy, but a *living* body's parts are interdependent.

Our interdependence is signed in our baptism. Once we have been baptized, we are no longer isolated and autonomous individuals, because we are baptized into the body of Christ: the *community* of faith. We cannot consider ourselves autonomous and still retain theological and spiritual integrity as Christians.

But this fact does not mean that interdependence is easy. In North America, true community is countercultural, it is "swimming upstream," because, as we have already seen, from our earliest days as a movement American culture has driven us toward autonomy. And in these postmodern times in which capitalism and free market competition rule the culture, community that goes beyond convenience and self-interest is even more countercultural than it was in the early 1800s.

We are talking about community based not on convenience or political expedience but based on *covenant.*

Most simply, *covenant* means "agreement." In the case of restructure, the agreement was that we would live together as one church in mutual respect with certain agreed-upon rights and responsibilities lived out under the lordship of Jesus Christ. We have a long way to go to realize this agreement. I'm not talking about the weak-kneed kind of "when-its-convenient-and-to-my own-advantage" kind of covenant that we sometimes see in this church. I'm talking about really committing to each other, throwing our lot in with each other. True covenant is not dependent on whether we happen to like each other or not. There is more at stake than just "liking each other." The gospel of Jesus Christ is at stake, the faithfulness and effectiveness of the church is at stake.

I submit to you that, in some regards, despite the wonderful language and concepts of *The Design*, we have simply retained our original agreement, which was a mostly political arrangement that seems to be summed up as "You cannot tell me what to do and I cannot tell you what to do." Unfortunately, in this kind of political covenant, Christ does not really enter the picture and cannot really tell anyone much of anything!

We do have a model of real covenant that involves Christ as well as all of us. We see this model every Sunday. It's called the Lord's supper. We are a people of the table! We come together at the table to celebrate the presence and lordship of Jesus Christ. In the face of a world that dis-members us in so many ways, we come to be re-membered as the body of Christ. The drama that unfolds before us at the table each time we gather is a foretaste of the messianic banquet. We come with all our differences of gender, race, culture, and sexual orientation. We come with all our hopes, fears, and anxieties. We come with all our differences of opinion, perspective, and experience. We come with all our hurts and pains and woundedness. We come with our sin and our brokenness, each of us utterly dependent on the grace of God. And each of us is welcomed there by the living Christ. We *are* made a *true community of grace!*

The imagery is there before us every Sunday, but often we do not seem to "get it." In our congregations, we can go from the table to the parking lot to gossip; we can go from the table to a congregational meeting to manipulate and emotionally bludgeon others for power; we can go from the table to a secret meeting to pull the rug out from under the pastor.

In General Assembly, we can go from the table to a business meeting in which General Robert (who wrote Robert's Rules of Order) seems to be more of an influence than our divine covenantal partner. We can go from the table to beating up on one another in meaningless battles at microphones that amplify our attitudes and hostilities for all the world to hear. We seem to think our business sessions are just a matter of doing business with each other (or *to* each other), forgetting that there is a third party present and that the covenant really means we are called to do business under the lordship of Jesus Christ, led by and in submission to the Spirit. Thus, the authority we honor is a political authority rather than a divine authority. Somehow we must maintain our reasonable suspicion of human authorities who *claim* the authority of God while we nevertheless *recognize* the authority of God. We must submit not to mere human authority but to divine authority—and we must do it together.

The Nature of the Disciples Covenant

The basic covenant (agreement) that lies at the heart of the Christian Church (Disciples of Christ) can be stated as follows: As people who have received the grace of God through faith in Jesus Christ, we agree to be church together, extending that same grace to each other and witnessing to that grace before the world. The important point here is that we are one people because we recognize our common dependence on the grace of God through Jesus Christ, not because we always agree with one another.

Most human communities are based on shared interests and hold together only so long as there is general agreement among the members in regard to particular matters. Each of us has been a part of many different social groups and organizations through the course of our years, and we have seen groups break up or divide again and again because of differences of opinion in one matter or another.

This phenomenon is not true only of mere social clubs and organizations. Throughout Christian history (and especially since the 1500s and the rise of Protestantism—"protest—antism"), we have seen the tragedy of division after division occurring in the church of Jesus Christ. In the early 1800s, when the Disciples of Christ were just beginning, most denominations were held together in large measure on the basis of the authority to enforce doctrinal agreement. One could be a member of a particular church only so long as he or she subscribed to the doctrine of that denomination. Denomination after denomination has been created as churches have split and divided over doctrinal issues. It is as though people have believed that salvation is dependent on believing exactly the right way about certain issues. In past centuries, those issues have included whether or not a real Christian can drink alcohol, or dance, or be baptized in certain ways, or how a real Christian interprets certain passages of scripture, or dresses, and so forth. Today, Christians continue to divide themselves on the basis of issues such as abortion, homosexuality, and the interpretation of scripture.

In part, it was exactly this tendency to divide over doctrine that gave rise to the Christian Church (Disciples of Christ). Thomas and Alexander Campbell, Barton W. Stone, and the other founders of our movement recognized that the church could never be united and effective if it continued to make doctrinal agreement the basis of membership. They recognized that salvation is dependent not on doctrinal correctness but on faith in the grace of God made known in Jesus Christ.

This recognition was often expressed in a slogan that was popular in those days: "In essentials unity, in non-essentials liberty, in all things charity."[6] For Disciples there is really only one essential: faith that Jesus is the Christ. All else is nonessential opinion. Opinions are not unimportant, but they are not essential. This is why when one joins the Christian Church (Disciples of Christ) we are not asked to affirm a body of doctrine. Rather we are asked only, "Do you believe that Jesus is the Christ, the Son of the living God?" Thus, the Disciples' contemporary version of the old slogan is "In faith unity, in opinions liberty, in all things love."

So, as Disciples, when we are at our best, we recognize that salvation is not dependent on holding the right opinions, but on faith in Jesus Christ. Period. Nothing and no one is ultimate except God. Not even opinions about the important matter of abortion or other matters of human sexuality are ultimate. For Christians, only God as made known in Jesus Christ is ultimate.

Unfortunately, we are not always at our best. We live in a culture that constantly labels and divides people according to their beliefs and opinions regarding various issues. The past twenty-five years have been marked by so-called culture wars, by single-issue campaigns and wedge-issue politics.[7] The attitudes engendered in people by these are often carried into church with us, and we find congregations and denominations imitating the division found in our culture. We tend to elevate our personal opinions to the level of "God's will" and then develop an attitude of "my way or the highway."

---

[6]Rupert Meldenius originated this slogan well before the Disciples of Christ.

[7]"Wedge-issue politics" refers to the practice of choosing one or more peripheral issues about which people have strong feelings and elevating these issues to the center of the campaign. Thus, instead of seeking to bring people together on common ground, wedge-issue politics seeks to win elections with small majorities by dividing people along hard lines on particular, and often secondary, issues.

As Christians argue and fight about every imaginable subject, the church of Jesus Christ continues to be split asunder. Satan could not devise a more efficient way to destroy the effectiveness of the church! Christ prayed that "they [the followers of Jesus Christ] might all be one...that the world may believe" that Christ was indeed sent by God.

The Importance of Living the Covenant

John 17:20–21 (Jesus' prayer on the night he was betrayed): "I ask not only on behalf of these, but also on behalf of those who will believe in me through their word, that they may all be one. As you, Father, are in me and I am in you, may they also be in us, so that the world may believe that you have sent me."

When I read these verses from John 17, two frightening thoughts immediately cross my mind. First, our behavior affects what others think about the gospel. Our behavior affects what others perceive to be the credibility of the gospel! This is a frightening thought, is it not? And we know it is true.

Islam provides an example. The Koran does not teach terrorism, but because a relatively few extremists who identify themselves as Muslims have employed terrorism as a political tool, many people of the Western world assume that Islam itself approves of terrorism.

When Christians are seen hating and cheating and lying and all the rest, it is a reflection on the one we call Savior!

Christianity claims to transform people into Christ-likeness. Paul says in 2 Corinthians 5:17, "If anyone is in Christ, there is a new creation: everything old has passed away; see, everything has become new!" This is no theoretical statement on Paul's part. He says, "SEE, everything has become new." His assumption was that anyone who is truly in Christ has been truly transformed so that a difference can be SEEN. Paul goes on to say, "So we are ambassadors for Christ, since God is making his appeal through us."

We are all ambassadors. The question is, Ambassadors of what? Are we ambassadors of Christ? It depends on whether people see Christ in us or whether they see something else in us. What people see in us is dependent on our behavior. Do we act like Christians or do we act like something else? When people who do not know Christ see us, are they drawn to what they see and thus think that maybe they should investigate for themselves this one called Jesus Christ? Or do they see in us the same thing they see in the rest of the culture? Do they see in us behavior that suggests that even if this Christ is for real, he does not seem to be able to have any real impact on real people?

It's scary to think that our behavior impacts and shapes what others think of the Christ and of the gospel. But it's true. As children of a "do your own thing" culture, we do not like having that kind of responsibility, but the responsibility comes with our confession of faith!

The second frightening thought that comes to mind when I read these two verses from John 17 is that, specifically, Christians must be *one* if the world is going to take seriously the gospel of Jesus Christ. It is important not only that we show forth our Christianity as individuals; it is also essential that Christians be united with one another.

This means, first, that your congregation is called to be unified. How is your congregation doing in this regard? It does not mean much for us to be committed to the worldwide unity of the church if we are not committed to the unity of our local faith community! We could be like Linus in the comic strip "Peanuts," who says, "I love humanity, it's people I can't stand!"

You know (or you need to know) that your congregation has a reputation in your neighborhood and town. It may be a good reputation or a bad reputation, but it most certainly has a reputation. Most people who are interested in finding a faith or who are interested in finding a church home are *not* interested in becoming part of a congregation that has a reputation for conflict and fighting. In our North American society, most people have all of that they want at work and at home and in the world at large. They are looking for the peace that passes understanding, not another place to fight. If you have a visitor who is looking for a place to fight, to exercise control over others, to get his or her own way all the time, then pray that such a person will pass over your congregation and go elsewhere. You do not need that kind of help.

Your congregation has a reputation. I know one congregation that had so much conflict they were known in their city and region as "The Fightin' First!" Who would be attracted to such a congregation? Who would be attracted to a Christ claimed as Lord of such a congregation? No one I know!

The point here is that the unity within your congregation is, first of all, an issue of evangelism. You will not be able to convince anyone of the good news if you are constantly living bad news.

Christians must be *one* if the world is going to take seriously the gospel of Jesus Christ. This means that your congregation is called to be in unity, but it also means that our whole communion, the Christian Church (Disciples of Christ) in the United States and Canada, is called to be one. We Disciples have always understood this at a deep level. We were founded as a movement in the belief that the church is intended by God to be one. This does not mean that everybody has to believe exactly the same thing. There is, as Paul says, "One Lord, one faith, one baptism." He does not say that there is one uniform understanding of the Christian faith. Christian unity is neither unanimity nor uniformity. We do not all have to see things exactly the same way in order to be united spiritually.

We Disciples have a great advantage in our covenantal polity because we have the freedom to allow the Holy Spirit to move among us instead of cutting off the Spirit's work prematurely by taking votes that politicize our conversation. It is one thing to engage in dialogue, the point of which is to learn and persuade. It is another thing to engage in debate, the point of which is to "win."

The genius of the Christian Church (Disciples of Christ) has always been that we recognize that God intends Christians of differing perspectives to be church together! The left and the right and the middle are called to be church together! If those on the left said to those on the right, "Go away!" and they did, the church would soon fall into the sins of the left. If those on the right said to those on the left, "Go away!" and they did, the church would soon fall into the sins of the right. If those in the middle said to those on the left and the right, "Go away!" and they did, the church would soon fall into the sins of the middle— which are mostly sins of mediocrity.

Unfortunately, we Disciples do not always do a good job of new member education. We are blessed to have so many people who come to us from other traditions. They often bring new ways of looking at things that enrich our life. If you ask these folks what they like about the Christian Church (Disciples of Christ), most will answer the same way: "We like the freedom. We are free to hold our own opinions and to follow our own Christian conscience." New members figure this out about us quickly. What we often fail to teach is that this freedom to hold our own opinions and follow our own Christian conscience is only half of being a Disciple. The other half is extending that same right to others. Thus, we sometimes find members who came to us from other traditions using their freedom in attempts to impose their viewpoint on the rest of the church. Of course, some who behave this way are, so to speak, "native born" Disciples. In any case, nobody wins a church fight, and the ultimate loser is always the gospel of Jesus Christ!

So I ask you, the reader, What are you doing to foster unity and wholeness in your congregation, and what are you doing to foster unity and wholeness in the Christian Church (Disciples of Christ) as a denomination? It is not simply a matter of institutional survival. It is a matter of our effectiveness in proclaiming the gospel of Jesus Christ.

Christians must be *one* if the world is going to take seriously the gospel of Jesus Christ. This means your congregation is called to be one and the whole denomination is called to be one. But it also means that the whole church of Jesus Christ is called to be one.

I do not believe this means that the church should be one big monolithic institution, one "super-denomination" that spans the globe. I believe that there is room for many different Christian faith traditions that express themselves in many different denominational families. But there is no room for enmity between denominations. We Disciples have always known this; it is perhaps our greatest gift and witness to the rest of Christianity. But I am afraid that we have been distracted in recent years from this, our "ecumenical vocation." We have become preoccupied with institutional survival in our congregations, areas, and regions, as well as the denomination as a whole. There is nothing more deadly to mission than preoccupation with survival. "Whoever seeks to save their life will lose it, but whoever loses their life for my sake shall find it." These words of Jesus are as true for institutions as for individuals. We must recover our ecumenical vocation and help the whole church of Jesus Christ be one if the world is to come to the light of Jesus Christ.

The great Indian leader Mahatma Ghandi had a great appreciation for the Christian faith and its values. In fact, he was so appreciative of Christianity that he was once asked why he was not himself a Christian. He replied that wherever the Christian faith is found, there are also found many different steeples, which represent the divisions over doctrine and practice. "India," he said, "already has too many divisions." Think what it would have meant to the world if Ghandi, the father of the largest democracy on earth, could have embraced Christianity! But our disunity turned him away. Jesus knew what he was praying for and why.

It is forever true that when we Christians make each other the enemy, we are helping the Enemy. So on what will our Christian unity be based?

Can it be based on doctrine? I do not believe so. It is good for us to discuss doctrine with one another, for by doing so with grace, we edify one another. But we are saved by faith, not by doctrine. Thus, we would do well to follow Paul's advice in his second letter to Timothy (2:14): "Remind them of this, and warn them before God that they are to avoid wrangling over words, which does no good but only ruins those who are listening."

Can our unity be based on unanimity in moral judgments? I do not believe so. Only God is good, and so none of us can claim that we have all the answers to the moral issues of our time. Circumstances and perspectives differ and will inevitably lead us to conflict and division if we arrogantly insist that we know what is right over against all others. Our individual understandings of the Bible will differ widely depending on our experiences and perspectives. This does not mean that we should not live with integrity by being consistent with our own understanding of what God would have us do, nor does it mean that we should not make the case for our point of view in conversations with others, but it means we must not make sincere differences of Christian opinion over moral issues an occasion for division. Over time the church comes to consensus in such matters (just as the church has come to consensus around issues such as slavery, which was once a matter of controversy in the church).

Rather than basing our unity on doctrine or morality per se, I believe we must base our unity on relationship in Jesus Christ. And I believe we Disciples have an important witness to the rest of the church of Jesus Christ in this regard. The basis of the Christian Church (Disciples of Christ) has always been relationship rather than doctrine. But it is not simply a sentimental relationship that seeks to be "nice" or easy. It is relationship with one another that is rooted in relationship with Jesus Christ.

Thus, the Lord's table becomes an instructive norm for people living toward unity. We are made one as we encounter judgment and grace at the table. The judgment is not one based on doctrine, but judgment that comes when we encounter at the table the living Christ, who convicts us of our sins and shortcomings. Then, thanks be to God, having been convicted, we experience forgiveness anew, we receive grace, and we are set right again with God and one another. Feelings of humility and gratitude are evoked in us, and we are united by the experience as we realize that no one is less a guest at the table than are we; everyone has a voice, and there are no "margins" at Christ's table.

The problem we face, then, as contemporary Disciples, is not that we do not have enough doctrine, or that we need a creed by which we can judge one another's worthiness. Rather, our challenge is to become more firmly established in the spiritual disciplines so that when we come to the table (and at other times) we are able, in fact, to connect with the living Christ and to experience both conviction and grace. Our common experience of these leads us in turn to community.

Campbell and Stone and our other forebears were not the great Christians they were because they had doctrines and creeds to guide them. They were great lights because they were spiritually disciplined and could thus relate to one another and to the world out of a relationship with the living Christ. They studied the scriptures; they had a deep and active prayer life; they studied the church's tradition (its history); they practiced stewardship and service.

Visions for the unity of the church that are based on "right doctrine" are negative visions based on doctrinal judgment of one another wherein one is never completely confident of salvation but in which one can only hear, "Well, you're okay so far!" Such a negative vision can never be sustained. It does not build up the body of Christ but always results in separation, fragmentation, and the disintegration of the church. Campbell, Stone, and the others knew this was the ultimate result of such a negative definition of church, and it is exactly what they were seeking to escape when they rejected the "fencing of the table" and left the Scottish Presbyterian Church of the nineteenth century.[8]

So we have this call as individual Christians, as congregations, as a denomination, to be agents of Christian unity, that the world may know that Jesus Christ was sent by God. Our behavior affects what people think of the gospel. Our unity, or lack of it, impacts the credibility of the gospel. We are called to live and work for Christian unity in our congregations, in our denomination, and in the whole church of Jesus Christ. That unity will be rooted in our individual experience of the living Christ and in our meeting him together at the Lord's table. There at the table we will together experience conviction and grace. There we will find the power to be gracious to one another, despite our profound differences of opinion about all kinds of matters, and to live the kind of life before one another and the world that will draw others to Christ. Thanks be to God!

Questions for Reflection and Discussion

1. How would you characterize the difference between a social organization and a spiritual organism?
2. How might you personally be different if you submitted more fully to Christ and the Holy Spirit? How might your congregation be different if it submitted more fully to the Holy Spirit?
3. How does one "speak the truth in love"? Is it possible to be at once bold *and* humble?
4. What difference might it make in your congregation if we Disciples moved from a culture of autonomy to a culture of interdependence?
5. In what ways do you see true community modeled in the Lord's supper?

---

[8]The phrase "fencing the table" refers to the practice of church officials' allowing only those who have met some official criteria to come to the communion table.

6. Are you an "ambassador for Christ"? What does this look like in your day-to-day life?
7. What is your congregation's reputation in your locality? If that reputation is negative, how can it be changed? If that reputation is positive, how can it be reinforced?
8. How can you, today, work for Christian unity in your congregation, in the Christian Church (Disciples of Christ), and in the whole church of Jesus Christ?

CHAPTER 4

A Deep Christian Spirituality

Now the Lord is the Spirit, and where the Spirit of the Lord is, there is freedom. And all of us, with unveiled faces, seeing the glory of the Lord as though reflected in a mirror, are being transformed into the same image from one degree of glory to another; for this comes from the Lord, the Spirit.

2 Corinthians 3:17–18

There is a deep longing among contemporary North Americans for a sense of connection with that which is the source of life and meaning (what Paul Tillich called "the ground of being"). This longing is a normal and necessary human experience because we were created with an innate need for connection with our Creator. But even many who are not religious, in the usual sense of the word, long for and seek this connection with the Source.

Contemporary life, with its hurriedness and harriedness, leaves us all with a sense of disconnection. The great Quaker writer Elton Trueblood was right in speaking of us as a "cut flower civilization."[1] A cut flower civilization, as Trueblood explains it, is one that is cut off from its roots, one that has no means by which to draw nurture and sustenance from its soil. This painfully describes all of us who live in this secular era of "future shock," of lightning change. Because of the geographic and socioeconomic mobility typical of so many of us today, we feel cut off from our origins (some of us have *deliberately* cut ourselves off from our origins), from that which launched us in life. We often feel like "dry bones" living in a desert land.

Thus, we hear more and more talk about "spirituality" these days. Sometimes it is within a context of "new age" notions accompanied by freeform music, crystals, and astrological charts. Sometimes it is within a context of conversation about the body's own healing powers in the face of diseases like cancer. Sometimes it is within a context of pentecostalism and "speaking in tongues." Sometimes, we hear the word "spirituality" used in a context of ecological concerns and in the men's movement. Sometimes it is within the context of a call for renewal in mainline churches like the Disciples of Christ. Whatever the context, we are hearing more and more references to "spirituality" and to matters of the spirit.

However, with all these uses and perspectives on "spirituality," the word by itself has little practical meaning. It is often used to refer to a radically individualistic concept of a "divine soul" or a "higher self," but often without any specific reference whatsoever to the Holy Spirit of the God revealed in Jesus Christ. Thus, one must be careful to say that a first mark of a faithful church is not just "spirituality" but a distinctively "*Christian* spirituality" that acknowledges and seeks fellowship with the Holy Spirit.

So how might we define "Christian spirituality"? I will offer this as a working definition: *"Christian spirituality" is a way of life that relates who and what we are to who and what God is as revealed in Jesus Christ and as experienced through the Holy Spirit.*

Who Are We and Who Is God?

"Who and what are we?" This is perhaps *the* question of the current age because most of the old signposts that used to tell us who we are have been taken down or are rotted away, covered

---

[1] Elton Trueblood, *The Predicament of Modern Man* (Burlingame, Calif.: Yokefellow Press, 1984), 59.

with moss, or point to irrelevant destinations. Since 1920 (what many observers regard as the beginning of the modern era), but especially since 1968 (the beginning of what has been called the postmodern era), traditional authorities of all kinds have been mostly disregarded or found wanting and thus discounted and rejected. This disintegration of authority has occurred in the midst of the assassinations of John Kennedy, Martin Luther King, Jr., Robert Kennedy, and others; the exposure of the hypocrisy of white America through the civil rights movement; desegregation; the Vietnam experience; Watergate; "Irangate"; "Monicagate"; the fall of several televangelists; the cultural disestablishment of the church; the disintegration of the nuclear and the extended family; the age of mass communication; the rise of relativism; and all the rest of the public and private traumas, shifts, and systemic dismantling of institutions and traditions we have experienced. We have seen nothing less than the unraveling of modern society, along with its faith in *inevitable progress and the fundamental goodness of humankind.* No wonder we are confused about who and what we are as human beings.

We of this era do not want to give in to the cynicism of one who has been "waiting for the human crowd to wander off a cliff somewhere grasping its atomic umbrella."[2] But neither do we see a clear way into a brighter future. Wave after wave of change has left us stunned and disoriented. In the face of the unraveling of the modern era, some have taken to calling this the postmodern era, but the term "postmodern" itself reveals our confusion: We do not know *what* this era is, we just know it is no longer the modern era. It is a period of transition, that is for certain; but we do not know if it will last decades or centuries, and we do not know what we are transitioning *to.* No wonder we are not certain about who and what we are as human beings— so many of the old cultural clues are gone or discredited.

In the face of the confusion and powerlessness we often feel in contemporary life, no wonder there have arisen so many "spiritualities" that claim that we are somehow connected to God but that never *submit* to the Holy Spirit, never really touch the ground, never really address the world as we know it—

---

[2]Lawrence Ferlinghetti, *A Coney Island of the Mind, Poems* (New York: New Directions, 1958).

spiritualities that want to skip Good Friday and move directly to Easter!

So how *do* we decide who and what we are?

There are some things we know about ourselves by simply observing how we interact with our surroundings and with other people. A sociologist, Charles Cooley, wrote about "the looking glass self."[3] This is his way of describing how we look into the faces of others to see their reactions to us in order to see who we are. We all do this and learn *something* about who we are. Yet we see more or less than is there because we ourselves see with distorted vision, and those into whose faces we look are influenced by their own internal distortions and neuroses. As the apostle Paul says, "We see in a mirror, dimly" (1 Cor. 13:12).

For example, think of how this functioned in your grade school days. Some of us were variously pegged by our classmates as "class clown," "cheerleader," "nerd," or "big man on campus." Such labels often have a profound impact on how we see ourselves and what we become. I went to school with a boy whose name was Philip but who was tagged with the name "Floppy" by his classmates in fourth grade because of his gangly frame and loose-fitting pants. By high school, he was known simply as "Flop." Think of the effect such a name must have had on him! Conversely, think of how encouraging it would have been to be named in the high school yearbook "Most Likely To Succeed." Such caricatures by our peers may be somewhat accurate or entirely inaccurate, but they *do* shape the way we perceive ourselves and thus what we become and who we are.

Of course, this phenomenon is not limited to school days. Throughout our lives we continue to be influenced by what others seem to think of us, how they treat us, and how they relate to us.

So there are some things we can know about ourselves by simply observing how we interact with our surroundings and with other people; however, by themselves, these perceptions, these "looking glass selves," are not entirely accurate and sometimes reflect gross distortions of who and what we really are or could be.

---

[3]Charles Cooley (1864–1929) was one of the founders of sociology in the United States.

Some contemporary definitions of "spirituality" seem to suggest that we can know who we are without reference to God, and many contemporary definitions of spirituality suggest that we can know who we are without reference to Jesus Christ or the Holy Spirit. Both my Christian commitments and my concrete experiences in life render such definitions untenable. From a Christian perspective, we are who we are in relation to who and what God is, in relation to what God has done and is doing among us and with us. God as revealed in Jesus Christ and through the Holy Spirit is the One to whom we need to look to see ourselves as we truly are and as we are truly meant to be.

> When the Pharisees heard that Jesus had silenced the Sadducees, they gathered together, and one of them, a lawyer, asked him a question to test him. "Teacher, which commandment in the law is the greatest?" He said to him, "'You shall love the Lord your God with all your heart, and with all your soul, and with all your mind.' This is the greatest and first commandment." (Mt. 22:34–38)

As Christians we are called to love God with our *whole* being: heart, soul, and mind. It is by loving God, surrendering our false selves (class clown, nerd, cheerleader, or whatever) to God, and allowing God to transform us into who God intends us to be that we become who and what we are made to be, that we develop integrity and wholeness.

Integrity means being the same through and through, to have oneness of being—not to be "this way" today and "that way" tomorrow, but to be the same everyday. Not to be one way at work and another way at home and another way somewhere else, but to be the same everywhere. We speak of God as being *holy,* a word that means "whole." In the same sense, we are called to become "holy," that is, whole, integrated, all of one piece.

Again, I define Christian spirituality as *a way of life that relates who and what we are to who and what God is as revealed in Jesus Christ and as experienced through the Holy Spirit.* Some things we can know about ourselves by simply observing how we interact with our surroundings and with other people. But because we are created in the image of God, there are some things about ourselves that we can know only by looking to see who and what God is.

This is also tricky, is it not? Just as Cooley's "looking glass self" has its distortions, so our perceptions of God are more or less distorted. The German philosopher Feuerbach spoke of a "cosmic screen" suspended in space, as it were. Onto this cosmic screen, he said, we project an image of *ourselves,* which is reflected back to us and which we then worship as God.

Figure 4-1: Feuerbach's "Cosmic Screen"

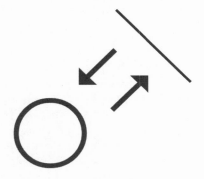

This is a masterful way of describing self-idolatry, don't you agree? And this is what makes discerning the nature of God, and God's intentions for us, so tricky: We are forever projecting onto God those characteristics we *wish* God had or that we have been *told* God has (told by other individuals, by religious institutions, by the media, or by other expressions of the culture). We subconsciously project an image of God for our own consumption.

But again, the problem in seeking to know and understand God is not that God is hiding from us, or being coy, or otherwise trying to make it difficult for us to know God and thus to come to know who and what we are. The challenge is in the fact that God is transcendent. *Transcendent* means "beyond the senses." Because God transcends the world and our human senses, we cannot see God in the same concrete way we can see our neighbor. Nevertheless, God is real and is made known to us through at least four basic sources of revelation and understanding.

The Four Basic Sources of Revelation and Understanding[4]

The first source of revelation and understanding is scripture, which for Christians means, of course, the Holy Bible (that is, the *whole* Bible, both the Hebrew and Christian Testaments). The Bible is the story of God's self-revelation to humanity through the Hebrews and through Jesus Christ.

The second source of revelation and understanding is reason and the third is experience. We Disciples are appreciative of reason and experience as sources of revelation and understanding. Our movement was born within a philosophical context described by John Locke this way: "Truth can be known through reason tempered with experience." In the secular age in which we live, I am afraid that many of us have increasingly depended on these two sources almost exclusively, sometimes in a way that is cut off from scripture. Nevertheless, reason and experience are two valuable sources of revelation and understanding.

The fourth source of revelation and understanding of God is tradition. By looking to the church's tradition (its history, its declarations, its collective wisdom) one can learn much about the nature of God and the nature of humankind. The church *has* learned some things in the past two thousand years (yes, the church learned some things even before Alexander Campbell!). As the sage said, one who does not learn from history is doomed to repeat it. Studying the church's tradition is a way for us to learn some things the easy way.

The Holy Spirit, which is the Spirit of the living God, uses these four sources of revelation and understanding to teach us who God is and who we are. But even this process of tutelage is one into which we must enter with great care, because there are lots of "spirits" in the world that vie for our attention and allegiance. Sometimes people speak of how God "told me this" or "told me that." This always raises caution flags for me because people who regularly hear disembodied voices speaking to them alone may suffer from a psychological pathology. Nevertheless, there is a real sense in which the Holy Spirit uses these four sources of revelation to lead us when we are open to direction

---

[4]John Wesley spoke of these four sources as a "Quadrilateral."

(and sometimes the Spirit "breaks through" our defenses even when we are *not* open to direction).

As we look down through the tradition, the history of the church, we see that many, if not all, of the heresies that have been identified through the centuries have arisen because someone tried to separate these sources of revelation from one another and from the guidance of the Holy Spirit. Although as Protestants we would affirm that scripture has a special place, we must not separate it from the other sources, nor from the guidance of the Holy Spirit.

By itself, scripture has been used to justify slavery and the exclusion of women from public leadership in the church, on the basis of Ephesians 5 and 6. This is the sort of thing that happens when scripture is used apart from the other sources and apart from the guidance of the Holy Spirit. Using isolated texts from the Bible, one can "prove" anything!

Just as we see ourselves and others through the haze of our own projections, we come at scripture the same way. We "read into" scripture our own experiences and biases. Because of this, we must continually open ourselves to scripture anew, applying our best thinking (reason), our life learnings (experience), and the reason and experience of the church (tradition).

Apart from scripture, reason, experience, and tradition, the "cosmic screen" can go into overdrive, and one can attribute all manner of truly unhealthy and unchristian thinking to the Holy Spirit. So we must keep all these sources of revelation together under the guidance of the Holy Spirit.

At a General Assembly a number of years ago, a resolution was introduced that sought to declare that, for Disciples, scripture is our highest authority. Upon reflection, I believe the General Assembly showed wisdom in defeating that resolution. Of course, the press had a field day with us through such headlines as "Disciples vote against the Bible!" But we were not voting against the Bible, of course. It was right and important for the Assembly to defeat this resolution because scripture by itself is *not* our highest authority: Scripture *together with* reason, experience, and tradition *under the guidance of the Holy Spirit* is our highest authority! All must be kept together with each other if we are to understand the truth about God and thus about ourselves.

In Philippians 2:5–11 (RSV) we read,

Have this mind among yourselves, which is yours in
Christ Jesus, who, though he was in the form of God, did
not count equality with God a thing to be grasped, but
emptied himself, taking the form of a servant, being born
in the likeness of men. And being found in human form
he humbled himself and became obedient unto death,
even death on a cross. Therefore God has highly exalted
him and bestowed on him the name which is above
every name, that at the name of Jesus every knee should
bow, in heaven and on earth and under the earth, and
every tongue confess that Jesus Christ is Lord, to the
glory of God the Father.

The goal of Christian spirituality is not merely to know
ourselves, it is to offer ourselves to God: to pour ourselves out,
to empty ourselves so that we may be available to hear God's
call and to respond, glorifying and serving God. Jesus, "the
pioneer...of our faith" (Heb. 12:2), was no mere ascetic who lived
apart from the world seeking personal enlightenment. Jesus gave
himself in total obedience and servanthood to God. This is no
self-glorifying, warm and fuzzy, "whatever feels good do it and
justify it in the name of spirituality" kind of life. This is the way
of the cross. This leads me to lift up the everlasting importance
of the spiritual disciplines.

The Spiritual Disciplines

My favorite definition of the spiritual disciplines is this:
practices whereby we open ourselves to being shaped by God. These
disciplines include, for example, Bible study, worship, study of
the church's tradition, stewardship, service, hospitality to
strangers, and, perhaps most notably, *prayer.*

Now, many of us attend worship regularly and many of us
are deeply involved in Christian service. This is good. But I dare
say that pitifully few of us engage in regular disciplined
stewardship that has as its foundation the biblical practice of
tithing, or disciplined prayer and disciplined study of the
scriptures and tradition. In the hectic, fast-paced lifestyle most
of us live in this postmodern age, prayer and study are

exceedingly difficult to do with disciplined regularity. And yet there is no substitute for them. There is no other way to deepen our understanding of God except through these spiritual disciplines, and because we have to know something about God in order to know some things about ourselves, there is really no way to come to know ourselves apart from the spiritual disciplines. There is no way to empty ourselves and to be filled by the Holy Spirit apart from the spiritual disciplines.

We Disciples do not much like discipline, do we? The world today reinforces our desire to "get something for nothing," to follow the path of least resistance, to read no book, to defer no gratification, to follow no discipline. Nevertheless, the words of Jesus are still true: "Enter through the narrow gate; for the gate is wide and the road is easy that leads to destruction, and there are many who take it. For the gate is narrow and the road is hard that leads to life, and there are few who find it" (Mt. 7:13–14). Jesus is not speaking here of narrow-minded interpretations of the Jewish Scriptures. He is speaking of living a spiritually disciplined life.

It is no accident that Jesus had studied the scriptures and tradition, no accident that he drew on reason and experience in his teaching, no accident that he was continually withdrawing in prayer. But, ultimately, the Christian life is lived not only by regular withdrawal for study and prayer, but by emptying oneself, being filled by the Holy Spirit, and then using every occasion as an opportunity to be a servant to God and God's desires.

So "Christian spirituality" understands who and what we are in relation to who and what God is as revealed in Jesus Christ and as experienced through the Holy Spirit. Although it requires solitary practices and disciplines, it is never isolated from the community of Christians, but serves to enrich the whole community of the faithful and builds *true community*. Through it we recognize the reality of evil, yet it inevitably leads us to affirm the basic goodness of humankind and all of creation and thus moves us to seek *justice*. It empties us, fills us with the Holy Spirit, and leads us to become servants of God. This is the *deep Christian spirituality* I believe God is calling the Christian Church (Disciples of Christ) to manifest. This is an essential mark of faithfulness for a church in this age (or any age).

Contrast this kind of spirituality with what we often see among the Disciples of Christ today. I do not wish to be overly negative, for I see much of value occurring in all three manifestations of our life as a communion. Nevertheless, we see too many worship services that lack passion and joy, or, on the other hand, that have little more than emotional content; we see too many worship services that lack authenticity and seem to be ceremony and ritual for their own sake. We see a people who seldom speak of their faith and who too often justify their beliefs and actions by secular criteria rather than by conviction of faith and the practice of a disciplined Christian spirituality. We see too many individuals, both lay and clergy, who are burned out or depressed. I confess that I have been there myself. I believe any honest assessment of our church's life would conclude that we Disciples are spiritually needful.

Such an honest assessment is exactly what Jesus calls for in the first beatitude: "Blessed are the poor in spirit." Or, more helpfully translated from the Greek, "Blessed are those who recognize their spiritual need."

We Disciples have always manifested a kind of "anti-pious" piety; that is, we have often defined ourselves over against the expressions of spiritual piety of other Christian traditions. This is not all bad, because it prevents us from "praying for show." But in a culture that is increasingly secular, *there is no predominant or commonly recognized Christian piety against which we can define ourselves!* This is especially true of people born after 1965. We can no longer explain ourselves to the public as "not like those people" or "kind of like *them* but different in such and such a way."

Therefore, I believe we must develop a *positive* spirituality that is not simply reactive, but that is *proactive.* I believe that we need nothing less than a *new* "Disciples spirituality."

A New Disciples Spirituality

What will this "new Disciples spirituality" look like? In some ways, it will look like our Disciples spirituality has always looked, but it will also be quite different.

First of all, I believe a "new Disciples spirituality" will be *reasonable.* Reason is such a core value of our tradition that I believe any authentically Disciples spirituality will be "reasonable." We have always believed that one should not have to "check one's brain at the door" when coming to worship. Nor should we have to do so when practicing the other spiritual disciplines. But, second, I believe it must also be *experiential*, which is to say it must involve the head *and* the heart, the intellect *and* emotion. Experiential is not the opposite of reasonable. The opposite of reasonable is *un*reasonable. My point is that it is not enough for us to have a "head-only" religion. We must recover our passion and our sense of personal relationship with the living God.

Third, it will be *relational*; that is, an authentic Disciples spirituality will not be merely individualistic, but will express itself in true community and in a passion for justice. We see this relational quality of Disciples spirituality expressed and symbolized at the Lord's table every Sunday, but many of us have forgotten what the table means and to what it points. We must recover the relational quality of our spirituality and the vitality of our celebration of the Lord's supper.

Fourth, it will be *ecumenical.* True Disciples will never be sectarian,[5] but will always seek ways by which to connect themselves spiritually with Christians of other traditions. Our belief in and commitment to Christian unity has a side benefit we have not always recognized. Because we appreciate the unity of all Christians and therefore the value of all Christian traditions, we are free to draw on and claim for ourselves the spiritual practices and tools of the whole range of Christian expression. This means we can utilize the insights and practices of Roman Catholics, Orthodox, Evangelicals, and Pentecostals. Although we must be careful to keep these practices and forms connected with their own contexts and to translate them into Disciples practice carefully and with appreciation for our own ethos, we can draw on them to enrich our own experience and tradition.

Although there are other qualities of an authentic yet new Disciples spirituality, I wish to mention just one more. It will be *visible!* As I said, we Disciples have always "bounced off" the spirituality and ecclesiology of others. We have always been careful not to be too "obvious" with our faith, not too pushy or

---

[5] *Sectarian* means the tendency to separate oneself from others, believing that one's own way is the *only* correct way.

forward. We are, after all, reasonable. This worked pretty well for us so long as we lived in a culture that carried the language and concepts of Christian faith, a society that assumed you were a Christian unless it was obvious that you were not.

But today we live in a secular culture; that is, while Americans still *say* they believe in God, most live without reference to God. Thus, Christianity is no longer assumed. In fact, although in most parts of North America it used to be assumed you were a Christian unless you said you were not, today it is assumed you are *not* a Christian unless you say you are.

I sometimes think that people could work at a desk next to the average Disciple for 25 years and never know that he or she was a Christian. They would figure the Disciple was a decent, caring colleague, but they might never know *why* the Disciple seemed like such a decent, caring colleague—that it was because that Disciple had a personal relationship with God in Jesus Christ and the Holy Spirit through that community of faith known as the Christian Church (Disciples of Christ)! *We must learn how to share our faith openly and graciously even in a culture that is often hostile to faith.*

So here are five qualities of an authentic, new Disciples spirituality: it will be *reasonable, experiential, relational, ecumenical,* and *visible*! And given the way the world is today, such a spirituality will have to be nurtured and sustained by the regular practice of the spiritual disciplines.

Questions for Reflection and Discussion

1. Do you remember being labeled by classmates at one time or another in school? What impact (good and/or bad) did these labels have on your self-image and self-understanding?
2. What is your congregation doing to help foster the spiritual disciplines among your members?
3. What have you learned about God through the practice of the spiritual disciplines?
4. What have you learned about yourself through the practice of the spiritual disciplines?
5. If you are reviewing these study questions in a group setting, share with one another how you personally structure your

time and responsibilities so as to provide time and space for the spiritual disciplines.

6. What do the people with whom you work and play know about your faith commitments?

CHAPTER 5

A Passion for Justice

*And what does the L*ORD *require of you but to do
justice, and to love kindness, and to walk humbly with
your God?*

Micah 6:8

*"Woe to you…For you…have neglected the weightier
matters of the law: justice and mercy and faith."*

Matthew 23:23

If any group on earth should have been sensitive to God's
desire for justice among peoples, it was the children of Israel.
They knew through their own history what it is like to be unfairly
treated by others, to be used by others, to be the victims of
prejudice and bigotry. And yet, we find throughout Hebrew
history that when they got the upper hand over their neighbors
or one another it was often necessary for them to be reminded
that God wants justice for all peoples. They embraced the notion
that they were chosen to be God's special people, but they
frequently misinterpreted it as being chosen to *rule* the world
rather than being chosen to be God's *servants* in the world and
thus to bless the world.

Those of us who are citizens of the United States often suffer from the same delusions of grandeur, for our own national mythology suggests that America was to be the new "promised land" and that we are "chosen people." To whatever degree it is true that Americans are a chosen people, I am quite sure that we, too, are chosen to serve rather than to rule. Given the human condition, a sense of "divine chosenness" can quickly and easily become arrogance and a justification for all manner of injustice.

Thus, God continually sought to remind the people of Israel that the desire for justice is at the very heart of God's self. Micah is not the only one who spoke this word of God's passion for justice. The prophets Amos, Isaiah, and Jeremiah and the apostle Paul carried the word of justice in their hearts. They spoke it, they pleaded, they begged, they stormed and scolded, they wept. They thundered the word of justice from the mountaintops, they whispered it in the valley of dry bones, so that the people they loved, the people whom God had given into their care, might understand.

Jesus taught that the weightier matters of the law are justice, mercy, and faith (Mt. 23:23). He lived and died that his people might understand that justice, mercy, and faith are woven together in the heart of God and at the deepest layers of spiritual reality. Thus, the Mosaic law was not intended as a mere pietistic formula for staying on God's good side or for looking good. It was given to be a web of connection with the living God.

I have come to the strong conviction that if we, the Christian Church (Disciples of Christ), are to fully realize our part in the body of Christ, we must attend to the words of Micah: "to do justice, to love kindness, and to walk humbly with our God." And yet as I have studied this church, I have become aware of the desperate dryness of many Disciples in our spiritual lives and in our community life, as we have squabbled and bickered and voted each other into corners. Most of us are not praying enough, and our community life has sometimes resembled junior high kids challenging each other to fight after school in back of the Dairy Queen. I used to think, *At least we understand social justice...we're pretty good at that;* however, as I have begun thinking more deeply about it, I have seen that perhaps we don't understand as well as I thought. That is, we haven't fully appreciated how these three things, community, spirituality, and justice, are inseparable. They are woven together in the depths of who God is and who we are intended to become.

Typically, we Disciples of Christ work very hard at doing church. But frankly, we are often not very *deep* disciples. Because our spiritual lives are dry, and our communal life is dry, often mired in a sense of powerlessness, insecurity, defensiveness, and anxiety about the relentless change that constantly confronts us, our justice-making also suffers from dryness, burnout, hostility, and a lack of grounding in the depths of the love of God. The more profound our understanding of life in the Spirit, of how the church is the body of Christ, the more we will reflect into God's world the deepest reality that God loves everyone: passionately, unconditionally. The truly spiritual life, as we begin to understand it, will lead us to a deeper love—of God, of ourselves, of those in our church, and for each human being in the world. The life of justice *is* the spiritual life. When we try to separate justice and spirituality, we cut ourselves off at the knees. When we separate justice and spirituality, *we drive a wedge between everything we try to do and the wellsprings of God's love and the direction and power of the Holy Spirit.*

If we are to take our full, vibrant place in the body of Christ, we must learn this: True community, spirituality, and a passion for justice are separated only at our peril. We must begin to live within this trinity, because this is the closest we can come to understanding what it is to live deeply with God.

What Is Justice?

Within this context, then, what is "justice" in biblical terms? As individualistic North Americans, we tend to think in terms of *criminal* justice. "If you commit the crime, you do the time" goes the saying. This North American thinking lines up pretty well with one kind of biblical justice, "eye for eye, tooth for tooth" (Ex. 21:24).

But as a biblical people, we must go deeper. As the Bible uses the word, there is more to justice than criminal justice, more than the punishment of individuals breaking the law of God or the laws of the land. Biblical justice also includes *systemic* or *social justice.*

We live in social systems—in marriages, families, churches, nations, and cultures. These social systems have a way of shaping us and our behavior, our perceptions and our choices. A "system," as I am using the term, is two or more people who are related to one another in some way. You and I are related because we are each a part of this system called the Christian Church (Disciples of Christ) in the United States and Canada. In fact, this church can be described as a system of systems, because every group within the church is also a smaller system that relates to the larger system. A youth group is a system; a Christian Women's Fellowship group is a system; a region is a system; a general unit is a system; a congregational board or committee is a system; a Sunday school class is a system.

As individuals within the larger system called "church," you and I make decisions differently than we would if we were not part of the church. The system influences our choices. People within a system have not only their individual desires and ideas, but also have the *system's* values and perspectives as part of the context of their decision making.

Marriage provides an obvious example. A married couple, because they are related to one another in a system called "marriage," certainly make their choices differently than they would if they were each living alone as individuals.

Systems provide us with support and resources beyond ourselves (which is one reason we relate to them). However, systems are human and are thus also subject to sin and to being used by evil.

For example, a few years ago there was a news story about a twelve-year-old boy in DeKalb, Missouri. He had been teased and tormented mercilessly by his schoolmates. So one day he took his father's .45 caliber revolver to school and later that morning he and a classmate were dead, victims of a murder-suicide. Now, I don't think that the children in this boy's class were what we would call "bad kids." On a one-to-one basis I seriously doubt that any of them would have so taunted and teased this child. But in the collective setting, within that system, they literally drove him crazy. Within the system that was composed of those thirty or so children, he became the leper, the scapegoat for all the fears and insecurities of the other children.

We have all seen this phenomenon, probably participated in it when we were children (and maybe more recently!), and have perhaps even suffered from it. In the case of this boy from DeKalb, it killed him. Individually, none of those kids were murderers, but we recognize that together they comprised a murderous system.

A second example can be found in Fort Wayne, Indiana, where I was a pastor for eight years (though I know similar examples can be found in many cities). The overwhelming majority of African American people in Fort Wayne live in proximity to one another, in what is sometimes referred to as "the black corridor," which stretches from downtown to the southeast edge of the city. This corridor has been created largely by something called "steering." Steering is done by some real estate agents when they are showing homes to prospective buyers. Customers are shown houses only in "their" part of town. Whites are "steered" toward white sections of the city, while blacks are "steered" toward black sections of the city. Although steering is illegal, it is also widespread, because customers are seldom aware that they are being "steered" or because they *want* to be steered.

The economic and social impact of steering is immense. As the black corridor grows toward a white neighborhood, many white people there begin to panic. Some panic because they are bigots and do not want to live among black people. Others panic because they believe real estate values are about to plunge because of their *neighbors'* panic. Others panic because some real estate agents go door to door to "warn" people that "*they* are coming!" Still others panic because they have heard horror stories about high crime rates in predominantly black neighborhoods. Some panic for all these reasons.

Because of the panicky stampede to sell, whites are victimized by dropping real estate values. Blacks are victimized because they are steered into changing neighborhoods where their homes will be worth even less than they paid for them.

Thus, predominantly white society keeps the poor and black confined to particular neighborhoods. Police departments sometimes begin policies that seek to keep crime confined to those same neighborhoods, which become havens for drug trafficking and prostitution. Unfortunately, most white churches pack up and run too! Often the quality of public services is diminished, such as the frequency of garbage collection and the quality of fire protection. In short, lots of people lose because of the systemic injustice of "steering." Many young blacks who see how this system "works" will, in their sense of frustration and hopelessness, turn to antisocial behavior. This is how systemic injustice operates, and it makes God weep!

I will offer a third example of systemic injustice: the crucifixion of Jesus.

Consider the many different forces and motives that were present. On the face of it, it is absolutely incredible that Jesus could have been executed as a criminal. Consider his teachings, his motives, his actions. There is nothing there to remotely suggest that he wished anyone physical harm or that he had any intention of leading armed revolt. Nonetheless, he was executed for political crimes, for inciting an insurrection. At least, that was the legal excuse.

But the *real* reason for Jesus' execution had to do with the fact that he threatened the system that was in place, which is to say he threatened those who were invested in the system, those who benefited from the system.

He threatened the religious hierarchy in Jerusalem. These men had an uneasy peace with the Romans. This is how the system worked for them: As long as these religious leaders kept the people quiet and made sure that everybody paid their taxes to Rome, the Romans would allow them to have a kind of limited governing power in Judea. But Jesus had been raising questions about their spiritual fitness to rule.

He threatened Pilate because people were getting pretty excited about this man Jesus, and if there was anything a provincial governor like Pilate didn't like, it was any kind of excitement that might lead to riots or other disturbances among his subjects. As the Roman-appointed governor, his job was to keep the system running smoothly by keeping order and seeing to it that taxes were paid to Caesar. If there were disturbances, he might well be out of a job, or perhaps find himself governor of the Roman equivalent of Siberia!

When Jesus was brought to him by the religious authorities, Pilate made a feeble attempt to satisfy Roman standards of criminal justice by pointing out that Jesus had done nothing deserving of death. But as Matthew says, "When Pilate saw that he could do nothing, but rather that a riot was beginning, he took some water and washed his hands before the crowd, saying, 'I am innocent of this man's blood; see to it yourselves'" (Mt. 27:24)—as though one can so easily dismiss personal responsibility for systemic evil and injustice!

So Pilate let the religious leaders have their way, in order to avoid any "rocking of the boat." As one reads the New Testament accounts, it appears the religious leaders were determined to kill Jesus in order to have him out of the way once and for all, so that he could never again question their fitness and authority and thus threaten their privileged position.

Pilate could have stopped it. The Sanhedrin could have stopped it. But here the system produces a classic moral failure of leadership. And the people? Most were apparently manipulated by the politicians into believing Jesus indeed deserved to die. They became a mob looking for a victim, a scapegoat for their own deep-rooted fears and insecurities. Indeed, they became another DeKalb classroom of ordinarily decent kids who blindly allowed themselves to participate in systemic murder. As for those who knew better, they, like Peter, were apparently too fearful to stand up for him.

There are obvious similarities between these three examples of systemic injustice. In each case, there is some self-interest on the part of the system. In each case, there is some selfish gain for those within the system—perhaps the alleviation of anxiety about one's own worth, as in the case of the kids of DeKalb; or perhaps financial benefits such as those accruing to those real estate agents who are willing to exploit the fears of white urbanites; or perhaps the political benefits to those in power or wishing to be in power.

In each case, there is unquestioning allegiance to a system on the part of most of those who participate in it. Apparently, few children thought of standing up to the systematic labeling of this DeKalb boy as "class leper." Apparently, few of those whites who participate in the initial stampede out of a neighborhood think to say, "Wait a minute. Who says this neighborhood is going to be destroyed? Who says black families are going to ruin the neighborhood? Let's get to know one another. Let's not panic just because some real estate agent says we should. Who stands to benefit from a stampede anyway but those who are trying to get us moving?" The crowd in Jerusalem could have sent Barabbas to the cross, a man who *deserved* punishment. But people are so often like sheep; in our fear we fail to think for ourselves. And systemic injustice always exploits our failure to think about how we are participating in it.

The Relationship of Systemic Injustice to Sin and Evil

Systemic injustice is not usually the product merely of one or two individuals deciding to behave in unfair ways. There is something more insidious about systemic injustice. It draws into its web people who would not ordinarily consider unfair behavior, and most often those who are participating in the system do not understand that injustice is being perpetrated or that they themselves are participating in it. So there is a larger kind of evil involved than that of mere individuals making bad choices.

There are three kinds of evil of which we need to be aware in regard to systemic injustice: accidental evil, individual evil, and systemic evil. *Accidental* evil is a matter of being in the wrong place at the wrong time in a complicated universe that has lots of moving parts. People who lived in Charleston, South Carolina, were in the wrong place at the wrong time in 1989 when hurricane Hugo came through. Few people would conclude that Charlestonians had been so evil that God sent Hugo to punish them. It was simply a matter of "hurricanes happen." As postmodern people, most of those reading this book accept this explanation.

Of course, how we look at it often depends on how we feel about the people involved. If a hurricane happened to hit our enemies, we might conclude that God was in fact punishing them (a rather uncharitable and arrogant notion). Likewise, if we personally live with a particularly heavy measure of chronic guilt and have not really accepted God's grace for ourselves, when a hurricane hits our home we might think God is punishing us (a rather egocentric view of the universe, considering all the collateral damage God would be inflicting on others in order to get at us). Most of us would ascribe such an event to "bad luck" or something like it. Such bad things just happen sometimes, even to good people. It is accidental evil.

The second kind of evil is *individual:* that which is caused by individual humans to themselves and to each other. There is not much mystery here. At some time in our lives, we have all done evil things to ourselves and to others, and we have all had evil things done to us. As Christians, we understand that we sometimes do this; we easily feel guilty about it and usually seek forgiveness from God and from those whom we have hurt. We also seek to forgive others who have sinned against us.

The third kind of evil is *systemic* evil. It is less well understood by most of us because we usually think of sin in individual terms, as *individual* acts of disobedience to God's law and will. We think of sin as an *individual* deciding to steal from the company or deciding to lie about something. This is one legitimate way of talking about sin, but it ignores the larger context in which our decisions are made, including the *systems* of which we are a part. Because individualism is so pervasive in our culture that it dominates our perception of the world, our political philosophy, and our religious thinking, it is difficult for most white North Americans to think in terms of systems in relation to morality. (African Americans and other racial ethnic North Americans have long understood the connection between morality and systems because they have been so often victimized by systemic immorality.) It is essential that *all* people learn to think about systems in relation to morality because so many of the world's injustices are products of *systemic* sin and evil, and if people don't understand it, they are likely to be used and abused by it.

As we have seen, we Disciples of Christ are among the most indigenous of American religious groups. We were among the first Christian movements to originate on American soil. Thus, we bear the marks of American culture, especially in regard to our individualism. It is a great strength, but when unchecked and allowed to become sin, it is perhaps our greatest weakness. Our church's history and practice are rife with overly individualistic understandings of faith. Our particular practice of baptism provides an example of our naively individualistic understanding of sin.

That is, we Disciples tend to think that in order to be engaged in sin one must be old enough to understand it and must actually *choose* to engage in it. Thus, we practice *believers' baptism*, seeing no particular need for baptism until one is old enough to have some understanding of the faith and to consciously *choose* sin (usually about the age of ten or twelve).

To put it another way, we usually think of sin as being merely a matter of individual choice, like red Christmas tree ornaments that one chooses or chooses not to hang on a Christmas tree. In reality, our sin is also systemic and thus more like red poison berries: They grow up out of the roots of the plant itself and are an expression of the plant's own essence.

In most other traditions of Christianity, baptism is practiced with infants. This is, in part, because those traditions understand that sin is systemic and that people are therefore in sin "up to their necks" from the day they are born (this is often called "original sin"). Later, as the infant becomes an adolescent, he or she is "confirmed"; that is, people publicly acknowledge their baptism as their own. The tradition of infant baptism followed by confirmation is therefore based on a fuller appreciation of systemic evil than is the tradition of believer's baptism.[1]

Because *all* of us live in systems, there is ultimately no way we can escape responsibility for the systemic evil our systems perpetrate. Take the system called "nation," for example. There is no nation without sin, and every nation participates in systemic injustice, if only because it is part of a larger system called the "world," which is itself subject to sin and evil. There is nowhere to hide! A person may wish to escape responsibility for the injustice perpetrated by her nation, but she cannot. Even if she chooses to leave her nation and goes to live on a deserted island somewhere, she cannot escape responsibility for what her nation does in her absence, since she *could* have stayed home and struggled against the injustice. Many of those who fled Nazi Germany in the 1930s struggled with just such a sense of responsibility and guilt because they wondered whether perhaps

---

[1] Nevertheless, I personally prefer believer's baptism by immersion for three reasons: (1) It is so powerfully visual; (2) it is an experience that a person never forgets (whereas no one remembers being baptized as an infant); (3) I trust God's grace even in the absence of baptism during those first ten or twelve years of life.

Having said this, I think one reason it is so important for us to work ecumenically with other traditions is because when we understand their history and ways of doing things, we get fresh and different perspectives on the faith that help round out our own. Baptism is a good example. Infant baptism as practiced by the majority of Christians helps remind us that sin is with us always, not just after we come of age, and it is with us systemically as well as individually.

they should have stayed and somehow struggled against Hitler from inside Germany.

Because there is no escape from responsibility for systemic sin (even though we do not *want* to participate in it), we are all utterly dependent on the grace of God.

The Current Social Context

Clearly, Christians have a responsibility, both individually and as the church collectively, to struggle against evil as it issues forth in both individual and systemic injustice. And the church's response to injustice must be made within the social context of the current day.

We are living in what is sometimes called a "postestablishment" time. When sociologists speak of "the establishment," they are referring to that largely informal coalition of white Anglo-Saxon Protestant movers and shakers that in many ways shaped the socioeconomic and political life of the United States from the nation's inception until the 1960s.[2] The so-called mainline denominations are called such because it was our members who constituted much of the establishment in the nineteenth century and the first half of the twentieth century. A list of these mainline denominations always includes at least seven communions that exist today: the Episcopal Church, the Presbyterian Church, the United Methodist Church, the American Baptist Church, the United Church of Christ, the Evangelical Lutheran Church of America, and the Christian Church (Disciples of Christ). Sometimes Disciples members are surprised to learn that we are listed among the mainline denominations, but the fact is that we have had our share of movers and shakers, including three U.S. Presidents and a disproportionate share of the nation's educators (in primary, secondary, and higher education).

But there is a subtle, yet essential, point to remember. It was not a matter of these mainline denominations *as denominations* playing a major role in the shaping of the nation's socioeconomic and political life. The point is, rather, that those who *did* such shaping were *members* of these denominations. Whether the mainline denominations, or even their key leadership, offered

---

[2]The story in Canada is a bit different.

much in the way of a vision for the society that was an effective, moral alternative to the mostly secular visions on which the nation was based is a matter of question.

I would like to see a study of how much impact mainline denominations really had in shaping what these WASP[3] movers and shakers projected into the national and world scene. I suspect that such a study would reveal that most of these movers and shakers were shaped more by secular forces than by faith commitments, and that those same secular forces were among the shapers of the mainline denominations themselves.

In the first two thirds of the twentieth century, there was a cultural hegemony enjoyed by mainline churches. Our leaders were welcome in the White House. More remarkable, perhaps, the White House often came out to honor the church. For example, President Eisenhower came to Manhattan to dedicate the new headquarters of the National Council of Churches in 1954.

But the mainline churches' cultural hegemony went far beyond presidential politics. Public schools avoided scheduling programs and sports events in a way that would conflict with church activities. Attending church was the accepted and expected thing to do. Protestant leadership could, for example, rally the troops needed for World War I and could prevent a Roman Catholic from being elected President until 1960.

This hegemony ended during the turbulent 1960s. The apex of disestablishment—that is, the disintegration of mainline American culture—is often pegged by sociologists and historians as 1968. This was the year when the number of U.S. troops in Vietnam peaked, the tumultuous Democratic National Convention was in Chicago amid scores of demonstrators and nationally televised riots, and Martin Luther King, Jr., and Robert Kennedy were both killed. By the time Jimmy Carter was President, just eight years later, the fact that he was a devout Protestant was regarded as a curiosity by the media. President Reagan was raised in a Disciples congregation but was a thoroughly secular politician. When he was elected, the door of the White House was slammed shut to mainline Protestant leaders.

Through the years, most Disciples leaders have supported the principle of religious pluralism in America. Many of us have

---

[3]WASP is an acronym for "white, Anglo-Saxon Protestant."

supported the arguments against mangers on the courthouse lawn and such other signs of cultural religion and Protestant hegemony. In doing so, what we hoped for was a nation where *all* religions would be taken seriously, which I believe was the spirit of the framers of the Constitution of the United States. It is ironic, I think, that what we got instead is a culture that doesn't take *any* religion seriously!

The bottom line is, mainline Protestantism has been sidelined and marginalized. We mainline Protestants have lost our easy alliance with the culture and our easy access to those in the seats of power.

So far, commentators have discovered no overarching characteristic that can adequately capture the essence of this period of history, and they have thus simply called it postmodern or postestablishment. But there are at least six characteristics of this period that have implications for how the church relates to this society in this age and how the church witnesses for justice.

Six Characteristics and Implications

First, *it is a time when nearly all respect for "vertical," or hierarchical, authority has been lost.* The Vietnam experience is a central cause of this loss of vertical authority. Baby Boomers, in particular, felt betrayed by their government because they were sent to fight a war of attrition that had no clear purpose or effective strategy for military victory. "Boomers" have not easily trusted government, or any other institutions, since. Those of Generation X (born between 1965 and 1985) and Generation Y (born after 1985) do not trust institutions because of the media's focus on the hypocrisy of particular leaders (politicians, televangelists, and others). This means that things must now be done horizontally rather than vertically. For example, few Americans believe or agree simply because someone says so. In order for truth to be accepted by most North Americans today, it must square with our personal experience. Authority now grows out of experience rather than position. This is at the heart of disestablishment. It has fundamentally altered the workplace, the school, the family, and yes, the church.[4]

---

[4]Canadian culture, and particularly Canadian Disciples, exhibit this same characteristic for somewhat different historical reasons.

Second, *truth is no longer regarded as absolute.* All humans and all institutions are now understood to be fallible. "Postmodern" means, in part, that no person or institution can claim to have absolute truth or to have the only correct perspective on a matter. We can no longer simply demonize "those" people or "those" systems because, at some level, we recognize that the demons aren't simply "out there" (in *those* people), but that they are also "in here" (within *ourselves*). For example, the civil rights movement was a lot more popular when we were struggling to change *laws.* Now it is more difficult to garner support for the movement because it must focus on changing *us,* and our *institutions,* where we have discovered that the roots of racism live.

Third, *there is in the land a sense of victimization, of powerlessness,* even among white males, many of whom must share power for the first time with others. This means that people feel powerless to affect what is happening in Washington or Ottawa or elsewhere in the world. In order to feel empowered and to have hope of being able to contribute to the realization of a more just society, people must have an opportunity to experience making a difference personally. This implies that there is a need for the church to involve people locally in a way that helps them see a connection between their expenditure of time and energy and real change. Most people want to see some results personally and locally before they are willing to go a next step, which may be a national or global issue.

Fourth, *this is an age of over-communication,* when we, and democracy itself, are overwhelmed and drowning in information and misinformation. Today, effectiveness in communication requires careful network building and sophisticated use of the technology. No one can build a successful initiative for national or global change on the basis of group statements and resolutions alone, as helpful as they sometimes are. It was by understanding this need to build networks and to effectively use communication technology that the group known as the Christian Coalition effectively captured Congress in the 1980s. However, merely having a large address list or e-mail list is not the same thing as having an effective network. Those individuals who are enlisted in our networks must have passion for the issue or issues, and that passion must be continually nurtured (this is why Bread for the World, an organization of citizens concerned about world hunger, has local groups to reinforce its communication network). The more complicated the issue and the more long term the struggle, the more important this nurture is to ensure that the members of the network remain motivated and actively engaged in contacting their legislators.

Fifth, *many people (especially younger people) are aware of global pluralism and value diversity.* Thus, the church must also be careful to respect diversity and must recognize the rights of all peoples and cultures. In part, this means the church must not simply pit the legitimate needs of one group of people over against the legitimate needs of other groups of people. It also means that the church must address the inequities within its own life and practice as a matter of integrity. "Justice" must mean justice for *all*, not only justice for *some.*

Sixth, *the media tends to make it appear as though everyone is lined up on the "left" or the "right" of every issue.* The fact is that on most issues most Americans are somewhere in between, trying to figure out what to think and do. Thus, when the church issues a call for change and reform, it must address both individual and systemic aspects of issues and problems. In the United States, it seems to me that the Republican party tends to focus on individual responsibility almost exclusively, while the Democratic party tends to focus on the responsibility of systems almost exclusively. Huge numbers of thinking Americans are moving away from old-time loyalty to either party because they know that the issues confronting the world have both individual and systemic components and that any effective approach to issues must address both aspects. It is the failure to recognize this need to address both aspects that has hurt many modern[5] social movements. Many old-style liberal organizations are struggling to make it into the postmodern era in part because they speak almost exclusively to systemic sin and injustice rather than also addressing individual sin and responsibility. Thus, they have lost much of their credibility. Conversely, many old-style conservative organizations speak only to individual responsibility and refuse

---

[5]In this sense, "modern" refers to social movements that developed approximately in the late nineteenth century through the 1970s.

to acknowledge that there are systemic components to the problems that confront society.

Likewise, even though most Americans do not generally think abortion is a good thing, most do not support the "pro-life movement" because it focuses almost exclusively on individual responsibility to avoid unwanted pregnancies while largely ignoring the systemic causes of unwanted pregnancy. Likewise, many Americans are reticent to support the "pro-choice movement" because it focuses almost exclusively on the systemic issues while largely ignoring the responsibility of the individual to avoid unwanted pregnancies. In the present climate of moral ambiguity, any action or program that does not call for both systemic change *and* personal responsibility will be rejected by most Americans as abstract and inadequate.

Although the media makes it appear as though everyone is lined up on the left or the right, the fact is that most Americans are somewhere in between waiting for someone to offer a balanced approach to reform rather than an approach that simply demonizes either systems or individuals. The church is called to offer analyses and solutions that appreciate both individual and systemic causes and solutions.

These six characteristics of this age and six implications for how the church relates to this society are essential for us to understand as we think about how the church can effectively witness for justice:

1. CHARACTERISTIC: It is a time when nearly all respect for "vertical," or hierarchical, authority has been lost.
   IMPLICATION: Authority now grows out of experience rather than position, so people must be provided opportunities for firsthand experience of injustice and solutions rather than simply being *told* what to think and do.
2. CHARACTERISTIC: Truth is no longer regarded as being absolute.
   IMPLICATION: No person or institution can claim to have absolute truth (even if their mission is to seek it) or to have the *only* correct perspective on a matter, so declarations and calls to action must address many differing perspectives.
3. CHARACTERISTIC: There is a sense of victimization, of powerlessness.

IMPLICATION: There is a need for the church to involve people in a way that helps them see a connection between their expenditure of time and energy and real change.

4. CHARACTERISTIC: This is an age of over-communication.
   IMPLICATION: Effectiveness in communication requires careful face-to-face network building in addition to sophisticated use of the technology so as to cut through the communications glut and clutter.

5. CHARACTERISTIC: Many people (especially younger people) are aware of global pluralism and value diversity.
   IMPLICATION: The church must also be careful to respect diversity and must recognize the rights of all peoples and cultures.

6. CHARACTERISTIC: The media makes it appear as though everyone is lined up on the left or the right of every issue, but most people are in between these extremes.
   IMPLICATION: When the church issues a call for change and reform, it must address both individual and systemic aspects of issues and problems

It should be said, of course, that the result of the dis-establishment of mainline culture, and mainline denominations along with it, is not all bad. The mainline WASP vision of America has often been based on privilege for some and flawed with bigotry, arrogance, and injustice. Nevertheless, neither the narrow vision of religious sectarians and fundamentalists nor the pragmatic vision of purely secular leadership has been more enlightened. Nor would be the reign of chaos. There is still a need for a vision of human society based on Micah's prophetic words, "to do justice, to love kindness, and to walk humbly with your God." Among mainline Protestants, this vision has seldom been that of more than a relative few. Too often, members and leaders of mainline denominations have worshiped at the altar of cultural religion, confusing the nation's self-interests with God's vision for the world.

In the United States, as in so many European nations in centuries past, politicians and other cultural leaders hold the real power, while politely and publicly deferring to the clergy so as to keep them from making too much of a ruckus or stirring up too much trouble among the laity. This may be overstated a bit, but not as much as we might like to think. Those in the seats of power have always recognized that it is when significant numbers of *laity* take Micah's vision seriously that the real threats to the kingdoms of this world arise. I think it is time to confess that we mainline Protestant leaders who are concerned for justice have sometimes been content to be "right" while also being ineffective in bringing real change to the world. We have sometimes been seduced by the "principalities and powers" (Eph. 3:10, RSV), with trips to the White House, rather than doing the hard work of actually teaching the faith and the values of the Realm of God (justice, kindness, humility) and motivating laity to live out these values.

There is, I believe, an important place for lobbying Congress and the White House; however, the basic work of transforming culture has to do with teaching and motivating laity as Christian citizens—citizens who understand the nature of justice and who, recognizing the ambiguities of existence, are nevertheless committed to using their "citizen power" and their socioeconomic power to see justice realized. The loss of influence of mainline denominations in the face of disestablishment is not primarily about the loss of members. Mainline Christians still account for some 23 million citizens in the United States. The issue is that these members often no longer vote or no longer vote according to the justice values that they have learned (or should have learned) in these churches. Many have begun to drop out of the political processes. Others vote narrow agendas that ignore systemic injustice and the moral responsibility of systems in preference for agendas that are merely about *individual* sin and responsibility (especially as it affects their own pocketbook). Few vote according to a moral vision for society that includes both individual and systemic moral responsibility because most have no such vision. This is particularly tragic in the face of the fact that there are currently few politicians able to offer such a coherent and holistic moral vision for society.

The Mission Imperative Statement describes the mission of the church this way: "to be and to share the Good News of Jesus Christ, witnessing and serving from our doorsteps 'to the ends of the earth.'" "To be and to share the Good News" means that the church is also the subject of its own mission, that it is called to nurture moral integrity and justice within its own life.

The Statement goes on to say that our imperative is "to strengthen congregational life for this mission." This is to say that congregations should be a sign, a foretaste of the Reign of God. The call to justice is nothing more or less than a call for true community where "shalom"[6] is realized. I submit that purely political strategies for the application of the gospel's call to justice, strategies that seek to impose a particular view of truth that is disconnected from the everyday practice of congregational life, shatter community and ultimately fail in the world because they have no credibility.

Those of us who desire true community and true justice must admit that it is only in the grace of God, mediated through a deep Christian spirituality, that we can sustain true community and the struggle for justice. To be lasting, community must be based on the life of the Spirit, not based on mere sociopolitical theories of one kind or another. We must therefore engage in more than mere ideology. We must engage in *theology* and the *practice* of community. Approaches that seek to "win" with no regard for someone else's having "lost" undermine community within the church and thus undermine our credibility *beyond* the church. People no longer respond to a vision that cannot be lived in some significant measure, for if it cannot move us toward a new way of living, no matter how "right" it may be, it is useless.

The Role of the Church

What, then, does all this imply is the role of churches like the Christian Church (Disciples of Christ) in the struggle for justice? To me, it implies at least eight strategies in public witness, action, and service for church leaders (including committed lay-people, pastors, teachers, and regional and general staff).

First, because the church is after all the subject of its own mission, it is important for the church to get its own house in order. This means, for example, addressing our own individual and systemic racism in our congregations and in our regional

---

[6]"Shalom" is a Hebrew word meaning peace; however, it refers not merely to peace as the absence of conflict, but peace as the absence of conflict together with the presence of justice.

and general life. It means addressing our own sexism, culturalism, and all the other "isms" that prevent us from being a true and just community. Apart from this, the church has little credibility, authority, or effectiveness. The "processes of discernment" that the church has undertaken are designed to help us face up to these "isms."

Second, it is appropriate for individual church leaders to give leadership in regard to specific issues of the day. For pastors and other leaders not to use their positions to witness for justice is poor stewardship of their influence. For me, this means in part that, from time to time as general minister and president, I create statements or sign on to the statements of other churches or other church leaders or other efforts that I believe are effective and credible. I sought to do the same as a regional minister and as a pastor of congregations.

However, it is important for ministers to understand and remember the different roles they play and how these interrelate. (1) Ministers are, first of all, *individuals with a Christian conscience* who, like all Christians, must be true to what they believe God is leading them to say and do. One's Christian conscience is nonnegotiable, and one must both witness to it and take responsibility for its content and for one's method of expressing it. (2) Ministers are also *pastors*, which means they respect the Christian conscience of others and take seriously others' legitimate needs. (3) Ministers are also *representatives of the body they serve*, which means they must be careful about the difference between representing the views of the body as they have been authorized by the body and representing one's personal views as though they represent the views of the body when they don't. These roles must be carefully and thoughtfully integrated lest one fall into the sin of arrogance on the one side or apparent lack of personal conviction on the other.

Third, it is appropriate for church leaders (lay and ordained) to establish and maintain relationships with local, state, and national politicians and their staffs and with other social and economic leaders. Such relationships with leaders holding membership in the Christian Church (Disciples of Christ) can be especially helpful, since they can become important partners in change. Church leaders can and should help politicians and other social and economic leaders understand individual and systemic justice as it is implicitly and explicitly called for in the scriptures. One of the reasons I chose to join Rotary as pastor of a congregation was that it gave me a relationship with some of the key leaders of the city in which I lived, because they were also Rotarians. That relationship gave me an opportunity to effectively address issues of import in which they had some influence (such as school desegregation).

Fourth, it is appropriate for church leaders to identify responsible ecumenical[7] and parachurch[8] partners that can help resource congregations and provide networks for education, action, and service. There was a time when mainline denominations maintained their own staffs of experts in various fields of social justice. Today, however, there are ecumenical means by which these needs can be met more effectively. So, for example, we Disciples partner with the National Council of Churches in the United States to address issues such as the environment and welfare reform. We work with Bread for the World, which is an excellent parachurch organization that offers an effective hunger legislation network in which individual members and congregations can easily become involved. Likewise, we work with Habitat for Humanity, an effective organization that builds housing for the poor. Congregational leaders will also want to work with and through local ecumenical and parachurch organizations.

Fifth, it is appropriate for church leaders to create and maintain networks within our communion that cross manifestational lines. Congregations, regions, and general staff who are working on similar issues and action should be able to communicate with one another quickly and easily. This has become increasingly possible due to the Internet. The Disciples' Office of Communication and the Division of Homeland Ministries are expanding these networks and have, for example, created a Rapid Response Team to keep church members informed on issues and possible actions they can take. Regions

---

[7]"Ecumenical" refers to those communions that actively seek the spiritual and visible unity of the church.

[8]"Parachurch" refers to organizations that are not actually churches but that seek to serve or work through churches.

and congregations can organize local groups that meet to nurture passion for these issues and to provide for accountability.

Sixth, it is appropriate for church leaders to engage congregations and individuals in directed studies that encourage members to participate in public witness, action, and service. The Christian Women's Fellowship has engaged in this kind of directed study for years. The "processes of discernment" also represent such a strategy.

Seventh, it is appropriate for the church to sponsor work and study trips to Third World countries. Such travel, as opposed to mere sightseeing, helps develop North Americans' sensitivity to the nature of justice and motivates them to become more involved at home and globally. The Division of Overseas Ministries can resource such undertakings. It is important that participants study the history and current religious, political, and socioeconomic context of those countries so participants understand what they are seeing.

Eighth, there is also an important place for groups within the church to organize around particular issues, to challenge the church to faithfulness, and to reinforce the church's witness from beyond normal church structures. However, for the sake of true community (not mere absence of conflict, but true community), leadership must always be mindful of authentic differences within the membership of the whole church when they are seeking to engage in and to stimulate public action and witness. There are great differences of perspective and sincerely held differences of Christian opinion around every issue. Groups within the church, such as the Disciples Peace Fellowship, have smaller memberships that are self-selected around particular issues and perspectives, and the leaders of these groups are therefore freer to speak for their memberships than denominational staff and congregational leaders are for theirs. Also, it is often possible for such groups to speak in a more timely way than can denominational leaders, who must sometimes await the authorization of a General Assembly, for example, before they can speak on behalf of anyone but themselves.

Such groups must recognize the context in which they operate, recognize that they are a part of the whole church, and resist the temptation to isolation and arrogance. In order to be effectively heard inside and outside the church, they must also avoid the *perception* that they are isolated or arrogant. Furthermore, rather than trying to get the church to speak with a voice that lacks integrity (for example, through General Assembly resolutions that are little understood or little supported beyond the assembly hall), I believe it is important that these groups themselves seek to speak *to* the church with integrity.

To be effective, churches and related groups cannot be perceived to be simply the Democratic or Republican party at prayer. Rather, all of us must help our members apply justice as a biblical value to their own politics and parties, weaving together individual righteousness and systemic justice. We must, in fact, help our members understand and commit themselves to a distinctive way of life that is itself a sign of the Reign of God.

I wish to close this chapter on a very personal note. I am not writing the following in order to brag (as you will see). I am not proud of everything I did as a pastor in Fort Wayne. But I hope the following story will help impress the importance of involving *members* in the justice ministry of the church.

Fort Wayne, Indiana, is a fine city in many ways, and my family and I thoroughly enjoyed it. As a pastor there, I was a community activist. I helped organize an antiapartheid organization and personally confronted the officers of banks that were selling Krugerrands[9] (including, ironically, a bank named after Abraham Lincoln, the Great Emancipator). I wrote regularly for the editorial page in regard to such issues as racism and the integration of Fort Wayne elementary schools. When Fort Wayne moved from an appointed school board to an elected nonpartisan school board, I recruited candidates, secured training in campaign methods for pro-integration candidates, and helped them organize. We won a majority of the seats and changed the district's desegregation policies overnight. I served as president of a group called Clergy United for Action, which made public statements and held news conferences around various justice issues. I served on the mayor's Task Force on Domestic Violence and in a number of other such efforts. When I left town to become a regional minister, the morning paper printed an editorial titled, "A Prophet Packs His Tent."

---

[9]Gold coins minted by the government of South Africa.

I am proud of all of these things, and I encourage every minister to seek similar opportunities for public witness, action, and service. But I have one deep regret about all this. Though occasionally irritated by my positions in regard to various issues, most members of our congregation were remarkably gracious and generally proud of their pastor's high public profile. And yet most never really owned *my* public ministry as *theirs.* As I look back on it, I made a name for *myself,* but I did not lead many members into aggressive justice ministries of their own. If I had it to do over again, I would intentionally focus on enabling the members' own ministries. I made the mistake of assuming that because *I* was involved, *they* were committed to those causes as well. That seems pretty stupid to me now, but it seemed true then. Today I better understand Paul's challenge to "equip the saints."

It was also easy to take pride in the fact that the congregation had started a food bank system that had since grown to some 22 outlets around the city through the auspices of the local council of churches. I thought that the many members of our congregation who served as food bank volunteers were learning about poverty and the poor through their contact with clients who came for assistance (and some certainly *were* learning about these things). What I realized, however, after spending some time with these volunteers, was that some were learning very little of such things. What was happening was that some were getting just enough contact with the poor and hungry to have their own prejudices and bigotries reinforced. They were doing effective charity, but many had little concept of the systemic causes of poverty. I came to this recognition late, so that it was only as I was leaving that we began to think about organizing training for volunteers that included instruction in the root causes of poverty and in sensitivity to clients.

It is important for individual leaders to model action for justice and to give hope of the possibility of real change, but not much will change in our communities so long as the church's public witness consists of a few individual leaders making a few public statements. In every community, we need to sensitize, teach, and motivate ordinary church members for service to the Realm of God. We need to provide concrete opportunities for them to act and to reflect on their action.

This is why I believe the most important role of church leadership is, as the Mission Imperative Statement says, "to strengthen congregational life for this mission," including public witness, action, and service.

As befits a people with a passion for justice, we Disciples should work *together* to create congregations that are truly alternative communities, that are safe places where all people are respected; where the moral ambiguity of life and our own participation in sin is acknowledged; where there is a deep Christian spirituality; where opportunities for public witness, action, and service are offered and nurtured; where people are helped to frame local and global issues in a context of Christian faith; where people learn about root causes of injustice and are supported in taking risks to do justice and to love kindness in the name of Christ; where people are empowered as agents of change in a postmodern world.

Typically, the Old Testament prophets spoke a word to people who eventually recognized it and were convicted by it. So much that passes itself off for modern "prophecy" is just angry prattling, sometimes aimed at people who do not know or recognize the Word of God when it is spoken in their midst. Therefore, let us cease merely "prattling" and weave together a church that manifests true community, deep Christian spirituality, and a passion for justice. Such a church will have world-changing power! Being this kind of a church is the most prophetic we can be!

Questions for Reflection and Discussion

1. How does the biblical definition of "justice" differ from the common, popular use of the term?
2. Name ten systems of which you are a part. How do these systems serve you? How do they use you?
3. Can you identify a case of systemic injustice that is fed by selfish gain on the part of many participants and blind allegiance?
4. Do the six "characteristics and implications" match your experience?
5. What additional strategies for public witness can you name?

PART II

Getting from "Here" to "There"

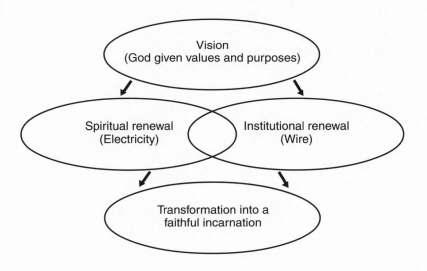

Introduction

We have explored the core values of a vision for the Christian Church (Disciples of Christ): *to be a faithful and growing church that manifests true community, a deep Christian spirituality, and a passion for justice.* I have offered a call to integrity and transformation that involves both spiritual and organizational renewal. I want to turn now to some of the specific ways in which lay leaders and ministers can embody spiritual and organizational renewal in congregations of the Christian Church (Disciples of Christ) and in our whole church today so that we might indeed be faithful and growing.

CHAPTER 6

Notes to Those Who Would Be Change Agents

The gifts he gave were that some would be apostles,
some prophets, some evangelists, some pastors and
teachers, to equip the saints for the work of ministry.

Ephesians 4:11–12

I believe every leader in the church today (lay and ordained) is called to be a change agent. We do not have to change everything, just the things that are killing us—the things that are keeping us from being faithful and growing witnesses in today's world.

I have said that, as general minister and president, my role is to call the church together around the right questions, providing spaces in our church life within which the Holy Spirit can lead us to solutions that transform us. I believe this is a rightful role for leaders in *all* manifestations of the church: the general, the regional, and the congregational.

The Interpersonal Dynamics of Change

Remember, lots of people like the current state of things and do not see the need for change in the institution. Some of these folks

87

just have a naturally low tolerance for change. Some may be among those ultra-conservative folks who think that "nothing should ever be done for the first time!" Others may simply have so much stress in their lives that the mere *thought* of change creates resistance in them. Some just like things the way they are—they aren't looking for a new and exciting mission; they aren't really concerned about what God might regard as faithfulness. They are happy with the church as it is, which is why they are there. They figure that if they wanted challenge and change, they would go somewhere else! They love it precisely because it *is* the same old place they knew as a child...and as a teen...and as a young adult...and....

On the one hand, all these reasons for resisting change have some legitimacy. After all, change in our world *is* occurring at a frightening pace, and why shouldn't it be a valid function of church to provide us with some sense of the unchanging, the eternal, in the midst of the temporal and the passing? On the other hand, God raises up leaders to keep the church moving forward. Churches are meant to be living bodies, not shrines.[1] So be prepared to meet resistance with love and caring, but also with firm determination.

Even those who recognize the need for change will find it stressful. Change *is* stressful by its very nature. The speed of change in our society has been aptly described by Alvin Toffler ("Future Shock") and others. Even when we see the absolute need for change, there is a part of our psyche that will resist it. Thinking of my own resistance to change, I recognize the need for learning new songs and hymns, for example, but I still don't like learning them! I confess that I groan inwardly when the song leader says, "Now we're going to learn a new one."

Human beings have an innate need for ritual, which by definition changes little. Ritual offers a certain kind of comfort in the face of the constant change in life. This is one reason why change in any routine, even the arrangement of the furniture in the church parlor, is resisted at some level by most everyone. This is also the reason why changes in the worship service rank

---

[1] In seminary, some of my friends and I used to enjoy singing, "Like a mighty tortoise moves the church of God!"

so high on the Richter scale of church change! All change must be approached carefully and sensitively.

This means that those who would change things must set a realistic and reasonable time line. As I think about the congregational conflicts I experienced as a pastor of congregations and then as a regional minister, I can see that one of the primary issues is often an unrealistic timeline.

When ministers are called to a congregation, they usually go with an idea of some things they want to accomplish in their new setting, and these most often involve change. Such change is usually good and needed in the new congregation, but it is unrealistic to think one can change *everything* that needs changing in one or two years. A five- or ten-year plan is usually more realistic than a five- to ten-month plan.

Sometimes when a minister is called to a congregation, the search committee will give him or her an impressive list of changes they believe are needed. But ministers should not assume that *all* their new parishioners recognize the need for such changes or that they are ready for them! The wise pastor will test the breadth of desire for change among his or her new parishioners before plunging into change that was presented by the search committee as widely desired. In fact, the wise minister will be "taking the temperature" of the congregation throughout the change process.

One way to lower anxiety levels and to create and maintain trust in the midst of change is to communicate, communicate, communicate! When people don't know how decisions are getting made and by whom, anxiety and resistance go up and the rumor mill starts turning. There should be open conversation about the reasons changes are needed and how they will be undertaken.

Get to know the history of your congregation. Just as important, get to know what people *think* is the history of the congregation: the *perception* is at least as important as the actuality. The past will need to be understood, appreciated, and taken into account as you move toward the future. Adolf Hitler was a frustrated artist and architect. He once painted a picture of a new Paris, but his painting assumed that the old Paris no longer existed! Likewise, impatient and heavy-handed change agents will be resisted at all costs.

Identify the people who carry both the formal and the informal power in your congregation and seek to enlist their support in the change you intend. Acting as though there is currently no power structure in your congregation will at least frustrate your plans and, if you are the minister and persist in such behavior, it will probably get you fired.

Identify the ethos of your congregation. "Ethos" refers to the ways your congregation does and doesn't do things: the kind of music used, the theological norm,[2] the social environment, the dress code, the kind of worship service (low, high, or in between), the building decor or lack thereof, the personality of the place, and so forth. It is rare for members to talk much about the ethos of the congregation, or even to be consciously aware of it; the ethos is mostly invisible. But everyone knows when they have run up against it! For example, in some congregations, a part of the ethos is that members are expected to bring their Bibles with them to church, in others not so. In some congregations, people are expected to say "Amen!" when they agree with the preacher, in others not so. In some congregations, the lay leadership is expected to be heavily involved in decision making; in others the pastor is regarded as the primary leader.

It is very difficult to change a congregation in major ways unless one also changes the ethos that supports the way things are. So if you really want to change a congregation, change its ethos! It is more difficult to accomplish than small, short-term changes, but the change will also be more lasting.

Be a non-anxious presence. People look to their leaders to allay their fears. If you, as a leader, appear anxious, the message is, "Something bad is happening or is about to happen!" On the other hand, if you are calm, the message is, "It's okay. This is all going to turn out all right." A calm and emotionally centered leader conveys purpose and hope. As you go about your leadership and encounter resistance, don't "fly off the handle."

---

[2]Even though Disciples congregations do not use doctrinal creeds as tests of fellowship, they certainly each have a theological norm—a generally accepted place on the theological continuum. Some Disciples congregations are quite conservative, some are quite liberal, and most are somewhere in between. A change agent who ignores the theological norm of the congregation will most often engender resistance and conflict. This is not an argument against changing the theological norm of a particular congregation, but it is a warning that one must do so carefully and sensitively as with all change.

Remember that you have your *own* need to change internally, you have your *own* rigidity. The things in others that irritate us so much are often those things we despise in ourselves! Humility, grace, and quiet confidence are as important to an effective change agent as are clarity of vision and determination.

The Current Generational Context

In order to lead effectively in the church today, it is essential that we understand this astounding fact: *This is the first time in its two-thousand-year history that the church has had to minister to six or so generations simultaneously!*

Biologically, a "generation" is usually described as about twenty years in length; however, I am using "generation" here in a sociological or cultural sense: A generation is a group of people whose formative experiences and worldview are generally alike. Thus, we have several distinctly different generations currently living. These groups can be generally identified as follows: the Depression era generation (born before 1915), the World War II generation (born 1915–1930), the Silent generation (born 1930–1944), the early Baby Boomer generation (born 1945–1955), the late Baby Boomer generation (born 1956–1965), Generation X (born 1966–1985), and Generation Y (born since 1985).[3] Of course, some individuals will better fit a group before or after them, but these general groupings are remarkably useful because they identify traits shared by most who share the same birth interval. As the characteristics of each group are described, most people find they "fit" their generational description in important ways. The members of each group have distinctive ways of looking at the world because of the events that were occurring in the world around them during the time they were growing up. A very brief synopsis of each generation follows.

The Depression era generation (those over 85 years of age) was shaped by their experience of the Depression, with its shortages and limitations. These folks tend to be cautious, appreciative of structure, and somewhat suspicious of institutions (they remember that the banks failed).

---

[3]Some researchers use somewhat different time frames and names for these groupings (e.g., George Barna refers to the World War II generation as "Builders" while some others refer to this generation as "Boosters"). The concept remains the same: People born in the same era share key sociological traits and perspectives.

The World War II generation (those 70–85 years of age) was shaped by their experience of that war. They have a strong sense of duty and loyalty to persons and institutions. They "saved the world" by getting organized and have been institution builders (some sociologists refer to them as "Builders") ever since.

The Silent generation (those 55–70 years of age) was too young to serve in World War II but were deeply influenced by it. As they were entering adulthood, the World War II generation was dominating the culture. The Korean War was theirs to fight, but unlike WWII it was described as a "police action." Small in numbers, and in some ways overshadowed by the WWII generation, they produced effective managers but not as many leaders.

The Baby Boomers (those 35–55 years of age) were born during a time of unparalleled economic expansion and optimism. They were told they could be and do anything they wanted, and many believed it. Nevertheless, they were deeply disillusioned with the Vietnam experience and have not trusted institutions since.

Generation X (those 20–35 years of age) was born during times of shortages and lowered expectations and so they tend to be more conservative than their Boomer parents. Many of them were raised in single-parent or double-income homes. Many were parented as much or more by peers as by parents. They place a high value on community and are concerned about issues but have little loyalty to institutions. Most have not been part of a religious community.

Generation Y is still quite young and so it is hard to say exactly how they will develop; however, they have been raised with computers and many spend a great deal of time relating through e-mail and the Web while being essentially alone. They are visually oriented. Most have never been inside a church and identify organized religion with what they see on TV (including televangelists).

This represents the barest outline of these various peer groups. There is much more to know and many resources available to help interested church leaders learn. Each generation has its own distinctive attitudes regarding spirituality, worship styles, approaches to Christian education, money, institutions, and most everything else you can name. Unless a congregation decides that it will seek to reach only one generation (and many congregations seem to have made this decision by default), it will have to understand and appreciate the differences between these various generations and develop its life and work in a way that is truly cross-generational. There is a sense in which this is a cross-cultural undertaking, because the subcultures of the various generations differ so much. Do you remember the example I used in chapter 1 of the missionary beginning work in the Democratic Republic of Congo? The first thing a missionary does is learn the language and customs of the people.

If we Disciples today are going to effectively reach the younger generations of North Americans (and North America *is* now our primary mission field), we must do exactly the same thing. That is, we must learn the language and the customs, the worldview and perspectives of these younger generations. Otherwise, it will be like trying to communicate and relate in English to people who speak French!

Each generation has its strengths, its weaknesses, and its temptations. I reject the commonly expressed notion that one generation is better than another. Each generation is different and each has its good and bad points. Any prejudice on the part of one generation toward another will inevitably become apparent in attitude and action and will limit the effectiveness of one's witness to the other.

Recently, in an elders' workshop, I was reviewing this challenge of ministering to several generations at once. We were discussing the fact that most of our congregations are predominantly composed of people of older generations and that the church needs to reach out aggressively to the younger generations. One of the elders asked a wonderful question: "Which generation should be the most flexible?" I responded, "The generation that has the gospel to share must be the most flexible, because we Christians are each called to meet those who need the gospel where they are."

The Maturation of Organizations

When I was first elected general minister and president, I read, thought, and prayed much (and with new urgency!) about our church's spiritual and institutional life and what is needed to move us forward. I discovered that movements usually start with charismatic, visionary leaders who articulate a vision that "catches a cultural wave" of the day, just as a surfer catches a wave that carries her along. Certainly this was true for the Stone-Campbell movement. Alexander Campbell, Barton W. Stone, and Walter Scott were each charismatic individuals who were articulating an attractive vision of church that included simplicity, Christian unity, and holding faith and reason together. This vision "caught the wave" of nineteenth-century individualism. Growth in the numbers of those who shared this vision was rapid.

But in order for a movement to survive more than one generation, there must be second and third and succeeding generations of leaders who can institutionalize the movement. History is littered with movements that died after only one generation, either because there was no one who was capable of creating an institutional embodiment of it, because the "cultural wave" it was riding fizzled out, or because no one effectively updated the vision to keep it contemporary and relevant in content and expression (this is as true for congregations as for the church as a whole). We Disciples are fortunate in that the generations of leaders who succeeded our founders were most often effective organizers who were able to create appropriate institutional embodiments of the movement. Today I believe holding faith and reason together still has appeal to many, many people, and the cultural wave of individualism is still going strong. Keeping the Disciples' vision both faithful and effectively updated so as to keep it contemporary and fresh in content and expression is a primary challenge that confronts us today in each manifestation of the church.[4]

An Organizational Maturation Curve

As they mature, institutions (including both denominations as a whole and congregations individually) follow what may be called an "organizational maturation curve." It seems that organizations of all kinds fall prey to what physicists call the second law of thermodynamics.

---

[4]Another challenge, of course, is effectively communicating to the world (and especially to the unchurched) that this is the vision we represent!

Figure 6-1: An organizational maturation curve

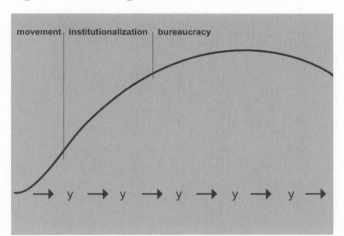

That is, apart from intervention, things just naturally wind down over time. This tendency follows a trajectory approximated by figure 6-1.

As an institution is successfully built, it grows in numbers, strength, and organizational sophistication. As time passes, the original vision/mission of the institution is continually updated by new leadership (line "y" represents this continually updated vision/mission). Eventually, a level of organizational maturity is reached that results in the creation of a bureaucracy.

"Bureaucracy" is usually regarded as a negative word these days (part of the anti-institutional legacy of the '60s, '70s, and '80s), but the plain fact is that bureaucracies are necessary to the accomplishment of some things. Large undertakings nearly always require some kind of organizational bureaucracy to be accomplished and for results to be maintained. The question, then, is not whether bureaucracies are necessary but whether a particular bureaucracy is more or less helpful. The challenge lies in the fact that bureaucracies, like all human systems, have a natural tendency to become self-serving, mired in obsolete methods (ruts), and preoccupied with control instead of with serving the mission for which they were created. It typically happens as shown in figure 6-2:

Figure 6-2

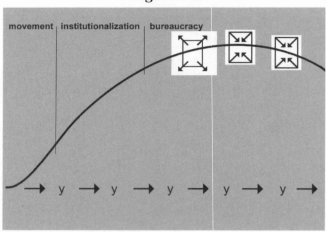

The boxes on the organizational maturation curve represent the "bureaus" or compartments through which the work of the organization (the enabling and implementing of the updated vision) is done. The problem arises when those working inside these boxes become less concerned about enabling and implementing the updated vision than they are about "life inside the box"! All of us have seen this happen from time to time in governmental, educational, social, commercial, and religious organizations and institutions. As the concerns of those who are supposed to be leading in the implementation of the vision become more concerned with "life in the box" (note the arrows that point inward), the institution begins to lose its missional focus (or the vision/mission is not adequately updated for the current day), it becomes self-serving, becomes mired in ruts, preoccupied with control, and suffers decline. Every expression of the church has this tendency to "turn in on itself."

Repair or Replace Obsolete and Worn-out Systems

A simple example of bureaucratic dysfunction in many congregations is found in the so-called functional committee system. I sometimes call it the "dysfunctional committee system," because there are often a significant number of these committees in a given congregation or region that do not function effectively for a number of reasons, such as poor leadership and unfocused purpose.

The functional committee system was introduced in North American congregations in the 1940s and 1950s in part as a way of involving the many new members who were coming into the church during and after World War II, and it was often very effective. The World War II generation had just won a war using such an organizational approach. They were (and are) good at it. It seems a natural and normal way to get things done to those of that generation. They use the functional committee system not only to accomplish the work of the institution, but also to get many of their personal needs met. For example, through participation in functional committees, they get some of their fellowship needs met as they come together with other members to enjoy one another as well as to plan and work. As these various needs get met, however, the length of the meetings tends to stretch out. It is not unusual in many of our congregations for one hour of work to require three hours of meeting!

The problem with this system is that, while it meets many needs of those who are of the World War II generation, it does not appeal to many of those who are of later generations. This is partly because as life has become increasingly hectic and fast paced in recent decades, those of the post–World War II generations find that they have less and less free time. For example, school-age children are typically involved in various sports programs, music and dance lessons, and other extra-curricular activities that require "parental shuttle service." More than half of all mothers are working outside the home in order to make ends meet or to pursue career goals that are an important part of their personal identity. People in cities live farther from work than did most young parents of the World War II generation and therefore must invest many hours each week in commuting. In addition, there are considerable pressures in the workplace to increase productivity, which often translate into additional hours of work. As for what free time there is available, there are many new and attractive options for spending it in recreation. Because of these sorts of time pressures and changes in lifestyle, the post–World War II generations do not relish the opportunity to spend an entire evening in functional committee experiences. In fact, it drives most of them nuts! In addition, because the lifestyle and formative experiences of these younger generations are so different from that of the World War II generation (and from one another), they prefer ways of meeting their fellowship (affiliation) needs other than sitting on committees.

Thus, in most congregations today, the functional committee system has become ineffective and inefficient. It consumes large amounts of time and energy and yields little (especially for those of younger generations), while creating the illusion that real work is getting done. As someone has put it, "We spend so much time and energy doing 'church work' that we have no time or energy left for doing 'the work of the church.'" These problems may be addressed in a particular congregation by seeking to impose clear agendas and reasonable time limits through leaders who are strong enough to keep the committees on task; however, it may simply be time to explore alternatives to the system itself.

The functional committee system begins with the assumption *that the institution* (the congregation, in this case) *has certain needs*, and committees are created to meet those needs. Thus, people are recruited for committees in order to fulfill the needs of the institution. Some newer methods start with an entirely different assumption—that *the members of a church have been given various gifts by God that they are called to exercise, and the institution should organize in such a way as to effectively employ and enhance these God-given gifts.*

A biblical basis for this gift-based approach is Ephesians 4:11–13, which is quoted in our church's Mission Imperative Statement.[5] As we read this passage, it is important to remember that when these words were written there were no "clergy," no formally trained class of leaders called "ministers." *"The gifts he gave were that some would be apostles, some prophets, some evangelists, some pastors and teachers, to equip the saints for the work of ministry."* Paul's assumption here is that God gives various gifts to *all* the people of the church. These gifts are provided for the work of the ministry, which is to be done by *all* the members

---

[5]See pages 4–5.

of the congregation, not by just one or a few selected leaders called "clergy."[6]

A gift-based approach to ministry requires more than merely changing the nomenclature of "committees" to "ministries" or "teams." A shift to a gift-based approach requires at least the following.

First, a process will be required whereby the congregation is helped to understand the shift in approach and the reason for it. Key leadership will need to be "on board" and will need to have carefully thought through the changes in church life that are likely to result from such a shift and the attendant anxieties that will be generated.

Second, a process will be required whereby the spiritual gifts of individuals can be identified. There are a number of spiritual gift "inventories" that can facilitate this. Choose one that is coherent with our Disciples ethos generally and with the ethos of your congregation in particular. Such an inventory will need to be administered by individuals to individuals, rather than simply mailed out or offered to "whoever wants to fill out one." Some congregations train some of their elders or other selected leaders to administer these inventories in one-on-one interviews with all current members. Then, as new members join, each one receives such an interview as part of their orientation and assimilation into the life of the church.

Third, counsel and/or spiritual direction is required to help people discern what God might be calling them to do with their gift or gifts. Carefully chosen elders or other persons appropriately gifted for this task should be trained and supervised (note that not every elder will be appropriately gifted for this task).

Fourth, individual members will need help in identifying and/or creating places of service for themselves within and/or beyond the congregation. This may be done by a leadership team chosen for this specific task.

Fifth, this shift requires the creation of systems for ongoing training, support, and accountability. Although a person may have one or more spiritual gifts in abundance, that person may nevertheless exercise those gifts in a way that is contaminated

---

[6]For a fuller treatment of this issue, see From Mainline to Front Line, especially pages 26–33.

by his or her personal issues, problems, and pathologies. Hence, training, support, and accountability are essential.

Admittedly, instituting an effective "functional committee system" would be a step forward in some of our congregations! But many congregations that have been experiencing diminishing returns from functional committees may find that changing to gift-based approaches will bring new life and energy. I have sketched a bare outline of such an approach here, but there are detailed resources available. (I suggest you check with your regional church office or with Homeland Ministries for suggestions and such resources.)

The larger point I wish to make here is that systems that a congregation or other institution of the church has used for years may have become obsolete without anyone's realizing what has happened. Perhaps the second law of thermodynamics has come into play, and a change of style is due. All institutions tend to get into ruts—familiar and comfortable ways of doing things that continue long after their effectiveness is diminished, simply because they are familiar and comfortable. In the case of the church, I like to call this "ecclesiosclerosis." It is not only a matter of stale approaches to organizational life. It is also a matter of stale approaches to spiritual life. For example, using the same worship forms and content over and over again may be comforting to some, but it eventually becomes deadly dull and ineffective for most. We all know the seven last words of the church: "But we've *always* done it this way!"[7]

Staying Clear about the Mission

In addition to obsolete or worn-out systems, another key reason the "organizational maturation curve" tends eventually to bend downward is because there is a tendency to forget what the mission is or to fail to update it regularly. This is a spiritual issue with organizational implications.

As I said in chapter 1, this church has had three primary mission fields. The first was the American frontier (from the early nineteenth century to about 1890) and the second was overseas (from 1890 until perhaps the 1960s). Now we must

---

[7]Or, alternately, "But we've *never* done it this way!"

address the primary mission field to which we are currently called: contemporary North America.

Look at the "maturation curve" again.

Figure 6-3 Maturation Curve

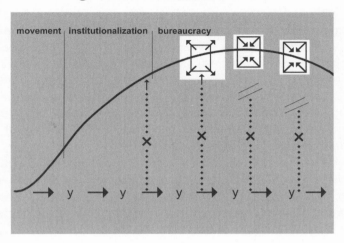

If line Y (the updated mission) is not renewed and strengthened regularly by lifting up the mission, in so many words, to the church (represented by the lines designated X) and reconsidering it from time to time, it will lose its power to inspire and lead.

Frankly, as I began my service as general minister and president, I felt that we had become hazy about our mission as Disciples. This is why I initiated the process by which the Mission Imperative Statement was created for our whole denomination. As a leader of a congregation, you may wish to initiate such a process of developing a Mission Imperative Statement for your congregation. You may simply seek to lead your members to acceptance of the general parts of the Mission Imperative Statement and lead a process that names the "bulleted" items for your specific congregation or you may wish to start from scratch (I recommend the former). Either way, I urge you to develop a statement of your congregation's mission that is consistent with the three marks of faithfulness (true community, a deep Christian spirituality, and a passion for justice).

Many congregations fail to serve their mission because the population around their building changes and they don't really want to address the needs of those new neighbors. Yet most members don't want to admit, either to themselves or to others, that they simply don't want to address the needs of these neighbors. Consequently, a congregation can become paralyzed and unable to do much of anything effectively. In such a congregation, anxiety levels rise as attendance and resources begin to wane. Conflict usually increases as well. The best antidote is to engage in a reconsideration of the congregation's mission and to honestly decide to stay and serve the needs of the new people or to physically move the institution to an area they *will* serve. The alternative is usually to watch the congregation continue shrinking until it dies.

A number of helpful resources are available upon which to draw in helping a congregation reconsider its mission. One of the best is called "Faithful Planning" and can be obtained by contacting your regional church office, the Division of Homeland Ministries, or Board of Church Extension.

Keeping Fresh Ideas Flowing

Keeping the mission clear and fresh and replacing or renewing obsolete or worn out systems requires an ongoing process for encouraging fresh thinking and inspiration. Why is it that some institutions are able to stay fresh and vital, while so many others decline?

Look at figure 6-4.

Figure 6-4: Possible Organizational Trajectories

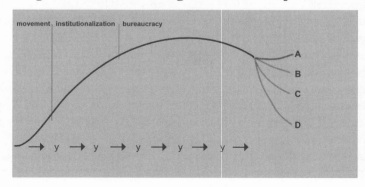

In figure 6-4, lines A, B, C, and D represent some possible trajectories an organization may follow once it reaches the point of maturity. Some organizations follow trajectory D, which means they decline until they eventually die. Since World War II, many commercial, industrial, social, and religious organizations followed this trajectory. Such organizations were unable to adjust to the new realities of the world and/or were unable to correct the internal forces (ruts, increasing self-service, and so forth) that led to their demise.

Other organizations follow trajectory C, going very deeply into decline until finally they awaken to what is happening and are able to change appropriately and to arrest their decline. Others follow something like trajectory B and are able to awaken, to change and to arrest their decline sooner. Others follow trajectory A and are able to engage in corrective behavior quite soon after decline has begun. Why is it that some institutions are able to follow trajectory A, while others follow B, C, or D?

There are many ways in which institutions protect themselves from trajectory D and foster trajectory A; however, I want to focus on one strategy that I have found particularly helpful. It is a concept that was developed at the Lockheed Corporation. Back in the 1950s, Lockheed called together a small group of engineers that became known as "the Skunk Works." These engineers were charged to think outside the boxes of normal corporate life. Some of the regular workplace rules were waived or have gone unenforced in the Skunk Works in order to allow maximum freedom and opportunity for innovation. The results of this approach have been fresh new ideas that have fueled the health and growth of the whole company. A highly disproportional number of the patents held by the Lockheed Corporation have originated in the Skunk Works.

I wondered, How can a church incorporate the Skunk Works approach in its organizational life? When I have identified a particularly vexing matter that seems to be contributing to the decline of the church, I have often incorporated a Skunk Works approach by calling together a dozen or so capable persons from across the life of the church, people who are representative of our various diversities. I ask them to struggle together with a particular matter over a period of 12 to 48 hours. Some of these people are selected because they have some expertise or experience that may be helpful, but I also select some who have no apparent expertise or experience in the matter being addressed so that they can bring fresh perspectives. In order to ensure fresh perspectives and in order to prevent too much ownership of particular analyses and solutions, I seldom call together the same group of individuals twice (though I may invite a few members to be part of groups called together to think about other issues). I commend this same Skunk Works approach to congregational and regional life. It can do much to prevent an institution from being victimized by those internal forces that contribute to "ecclesiosclerosis" and help it renew itself.

The Style of Leadership

One of the most important issues in change agency is understanding the style of leadership in a congregation. Arlin Rauthauge developed a very helpful description of four basic types of churches based upon their operative leadership style. I commend them to you for your consideration.[8] The four types of churches are the family church, the pastor-centered church, the program-centered church, and the corporate church. As I describe these four types below, I am using somewhat different numbers than those used by Arlin Rauthauge because of my own experience of how these categories play out among Disciples.

Our Disciples form of church organization is a kind of modified congregational polity (which I call "covenantal polity"). This form of organization tends to favor the family church style and the pastor-centered style. The family church tends to be led by a patriarch and/or matriarch and usually has fewer than seventy-five participating members. The pastor-centered church is one in which, as the name implies, everything that happens in the life of the institution must be approved or facilitated by the pastor. These congregations tend to have participating memberships of between seventy-five and five hundred. This is a key reason, I believe, why Disciples congregations tend to have difficulty breaking through the five hundred participating member

---

[8]A number of books have been written based on this analysis of congregations. I especially commend to you *The In Between Church* by Alice Mann (Bethesda, Md.: Alban Institute, 1998).

barrier, even if they are located in densely populated areas. The family church model tends to limit how much activity and creativity can occur in a congregation because everything tends to be geared toward the existing congregation, "the family," rather than toward mission beyond the congregation. The pastor-centered model has a tendency to limit how much activity and creativity can occur in a congregation, because the pastor can touch only so much.

Congregations that are larger than five hundred participating members often find it challenging to find a pastor who understands the need for a leadership style that goes beyond, and whose personal leadership style actually goes beyond, that of the pastor-centered church. If a congregation of more than five hundred participating members calls a pastor who operates with a pastor-centered style, one of two things will inevitably happen: (1) the pastor will learn how to do ministry in a different and appropriate style, or (2) the congregation will shrink to five hundred participating members, a size that is manageable with a pastor-centered style.

However, I would like to offer another category that I believe can function in all sizes of congregations and that will lead to spiritual as well as numerical growth. I call this a leader-centered style. "Leader-centered" does *not* mean that there is only one leader (a pastor, a matriarch, or a patriarch) who leads. It means that all kinds of leaders are developed. In this model the pastor makes identifying, enlisting, and equipping leaders a primary emphasis of her ministry. I usually recommend that the minister begin with the elected elders of the congregation, helping them to become better educated in the faith and better trained leaders. As the elders become well-formed leaders who exercise their gifts effectively and responsibly, others within the congregation are identified and trained for leadership and/or other forms of ministry (depending on their gifts). Over the course of a few years, the congregation is strengthened and deepened and the missional focus of the congregation moves outside the limits of its own fellowship.

Some who are reading this are lay leaders and some are ministers. I believe both are called to be change agents. It is absolutely essential that lay leaders and ministers share a sense of vision and direction and that each plays complementary roles with the other. Perhaps the worst thing that can happen to a congregation is when the minister(s) and the lay leaders are pulling in different directions and/or are in competition with one another!

One way to be certain that everyone is on the same page is to use a consultant to work with the congregation's key leadership and to help them arrive at a common vision and complementary approaches. Such a consultant may be a regional minister, general church staff person, consultant with an effective parachurch organization such as the Alban Institute, or private consultant. Whoever the consultant is, his or her role is not to manipulate the leadership to arrive at the consultant's predetermined notion of what a particular congregation should become. Rather, the consultant's primary role is to provide a *process* through which the congregation's own leadership can together discern and surface a common sense of vision and direction. As important, it is essential to develop a plan of implementation that will give the vision "legs." Otherwise, the vision will end up on a shelf, like self-studies so often do, yet another exercise in "navel gazing."

Maintain the Spiritual Disciplines

As congregational leadership moves through the change processes, it is important that the spiritual disciplines be maintained by leadership, both personally and corporately. How does a congregation's leadership engage in corporate spiritual discipline? The most obvious example is being in Sunday morning worship together regularly. But it is also possible to set the work of the board or other primary leadership groups in a context of worship rather than in a context of Robert's Rules of Order.

In the general manifestation, we have been using an approach developed by Charles Olsen called "worshipful work."[9] I commend this approach to you. For example, our General Board meetings used to be conducted as business meetings much like one would expect to find in Congress or Parliament. Now, we have a round communion table at the center of the podium

[9]Charles M. Olsen has written a number of books, including *Transforming Church Boards into Communities of Spiritual Leaders* (Bethesda, Md.: Alban Institute, 1995).

(created with a standard 8-foot banquet table that is appropriately covered and decorated). In fact, the note stand or "half-lectern" used by the moderator is most often resting on the communion table. We begin with singing and worship. What is more unusual, perhaps, is that we pause along the way during our business to offer prayers of thanksgiving, intercession, and so forth as relates to particular business items. We sometimes pause to sing a hymn. The moderator decides when these prayers and songs will occur (with occasional promptings from others). Sometimes we develop litanies for use with receiving reports, nominating committee reports, and other items. This approach helps everyone remember that we are first and foremost people who are seeking to be a faithful and growing church that manifests true community, a deep Christian spirituality, and a passion for justice.

Questions for Reflection and Discussion

1. How has your own experience compared to the issues raised in the section titled "The Interpersonal Dynamics of Change" (pp. 87–91)?
2. How many generations can you identify within your congregation, and how do they differ from one another in their outlook and spiritual needs?
3. Draw an organizational maturation curve for your congregation (you may need the help of others to accomplish this). What have been the significant points of change?
4. Has your congregation ever done a self-study using an outside consultant? If so, what became of the results of that self-study and why?
5. How does your congregation seek to maintain the spiritual disciplines as it goes about its institutional work and life?

CHAPTER 7

2020 Vision for the Christian Church (Disciples of Christ)

To Be a Faithful, Growing Church That Manifests True Community, a Deep Christian Spirituality, and a Passion for Justice

> *And Jesus came and said to them, "All authority in heaven and on earth has been given to me. Go therefore and make disciples of all nations."*
> Matthew 28:18–19 (RSV)

Faithful

There are a great many temptations facing the church today. One of the foremost is the temptation to sacrifice quality in the name of quantity. In the face of shrinking numbers of congregations, members, and resources, it is tempting for each manifestation to focus on strategies that merely seek to ensure survival or that are concerned with numerical growth only, without also paying attention to the quality of our church's life and witness. Thus, we Disciples could grow numerically while losing our soul! This is particularly tempting in an age of marketing. Integrity (faithfulness) must be our first measure of transformation. What does faithfulness look like? In this writing, I have sought to define it in terms of three marks: true community, a deep Christian spirituality, and a passion for justice.

True Community

In order to be faithful, we must manifest true community in our life together as a church.

Such true community will be based in covenant. *The Design* of the Christian Church (Disciples of Christ) is based on covenant, but we have not always fulfilled this vision of covenantal life. Living covenantally means moving from the culture of autonomy that is so common in North American society and in this church to a culture of interdependence.

We see covenantal life modeled every Sunday in Disciples congregations at the Lord's table. At the table we remember and celebrate the presence and lordship of Jesus Christ. We come with all our hopes, fears, and anxieties; with all our differences of opinion, perspective, and experience; with all our differences of gender, race, culture, and orientation; with our hurts and pain and woundedness; with our sin and brokenness. There we are welcomed by the living Christ, and we are made a *true community of grace.* In the face of a world that dis-members us in so many ways, we come to be re-membered as the Body of Christ. As people who have received the grace of God through faith in Jesus Christ, we agree to be church together, extending that same grace to each other and witnessing to that grace before the world. We are one people not because we always agree with one another, but because we recognize our common dependence on the grace of God through Jesus Christ.

This, then, is crucial to our being a true community in our congregations, our regions, and our general church life: to make our common dependence on grace the glue that binds us together, rather than agreement on doctrine or on various controversial issues, while actively engaging one another in discussion of those very issues and differences that would dis-member us. This is a daunting challenge and is possible only by God's grace and power, which points again to the need for spiritual discipline and maturity. Thus, we seek to live Christian unity both for the *sake* of the gospel ("that the world may know") and by the *power* of the gospel. And so true community itself is a spiritual discipline!

Such true community does not come easily or even naturally. Most people assume that our Disciples sense of community comes from agreement in various matters (though they are quickly disabused of this assumption once they have experienced a congregational board meeting or a General Assembly business meeting). Thus, we need to do a better job of teaching new Disciples our ethos and the basis for our life together. We must teach that our sense of community comes ultimately from our common confession that "In Christ God was reconciling the world to himself...and entrusting the message of reconciliation to us." We must teach that it is not easy to be a Disciple, because there is no one telling us exactly what to believe and what to do. It is not easy to be a Disciple because we are responsible for our own spiritual maturity and discipline. It is as we take responsibility for our own spiritual life and journey that, having accepted God's grace made known in Jesus Christ, we are able to remain in covenantal community with people who serve the same Christ but who are different from us and who view various matters differently from us.

A Deep Christian Spirituality

In order to be faithful, we must cultivate and practice a deep Christian spirituality. This means:

First, *as we seek to understand the faith and its call on us, we hold together the four primary sources of revelation and understanding: the scriptures, reason, experience, and tradition.* In order to do this, we will have to teach the content of the scriptures and provide people with some tools by which they can understand and interpret them. We will also have to teach the church's tradition (history), something we have not done very well in most of our congregations. This teaching must be done in a dialogical way that helps individual Disciples integrate their reason and experience with what they are learning about history and the scriptures. Likewise, our preaching must reflect all four primary sources of revelation and understanding.

Second, *we will teach and practice the spiritual disciplines,* which I have defined as practices whereby we open ourselves to being shaped by God. These disciplines include (but are not limited to) Bible study, worship, study of the church's tradition, stewardship, service, hospitality to strangers, and, perhaps most notably, prayer. It is not only in the congregations that we must teach the spiritual disciplines, but in our seminaries as well.

Third, *it is essential for the transformation of this church that our ministers become spiritual leaders.* This may be so obvious to most lay members as to seem pointless to mention; however, there are many models other than "spiritual leader" that beckon to ministers these days. Some of us ministers have bought into a C.E.O. (chief executive officer) model. Although there is "executive" work that must be done by ministers, and we need to do it well, that which is most needed of our ministers in congregations, regions, and general life is spiritual leadership. Some of us have chosen a "pastoral counselor" model, and there is a great need for pastoral counseling and psychotherapy among many of our members; however, I believe the wise pastor will refer such members to a regular practicing pastoral counselor or psychotherapist as soon as possible. Ministers need to focus especially on the one thing they can provide that no one else can provide, or cannot provide in the same way: spiritual leadership.

Fourth, *we will develop a new Disciples spirituality that will be reasonable, experiential, relational, ecumenical, and **visible**.* In a culture that has become indifferent and even openly hostile to faith, we must learn how to share our faith openly and graciously.

The point of all this is to move closer to God in our daily lives, to be more attuned to God's leading, to submit ourselves to the Holy Spirit. This is what deep Christian spirituality is.

A Passion for Justice

In order to be faithful, we must manifest a passion for justice within our church and within the world. Jesus describes justice as one of the "weightier matters" (Mt. 23:23). This means, in part, that we must help our members and leaders understand the structures of society, the "systems" that rule the world day-to-day, and how these systems interact with evil. It is essential that we learn to think about systems in relation to morality because so many of the world's injustices are the product of *systemic* sin and evil, and if we don't understand it, we are likely to be used and abused by it.

The church needs to address justice issues, keeping in mind the eight strategies addressed in chapter 6:

1. Because the church is the subject of its own mission, it is important for the church to get its own house in order. It is difficult for the church to address the injustices of the world so long as it is participating in those injustices itself. This means addressing racism, sexism, or any other prejudicial attitudes within our church life that cause us to exclude certain people or that otherwise prevent us from being true community.

2. It is appropriate for pastors and other church leaders to give leadership in regard to specific issues of the day. This may mean making public statements, being involved in organized efforts regarding particular issues, or otherwise addressing justice matters as an individual Christian, as a pastor, and/or as a representative of the body.

3. It is appropriate to establish and maintain relationships with political and social leaders for the sake of influencing their decisions for the sake of justice.

4. It is appropriate to identify helpful ecumenical and parachurch organizations that can assist individuals, the congregation, and the whole church in witnessing for justice locally, nationally, and internationally.

5. It is appropriate to create and maintain networks across the life of the congregation and beyond to keep members informed of developments and how they can engage issues.

6. It is appropriate to offer directed studies in particular issues.

7. It is appropriate to sponsor work and study trips to sites where justice issues can be seen, expressed, and addressed.

8. It is appropriate for groups of individuals to organize around particular issues. Thus, for example, within a congregation, those concerned about hunger may organize a local Bread for the World group. Within the wider church, too, individuals and congregations may organize for study and action.[1]

---

[1] An example of this is the Disciples Peace Fellowship.

Offering these kinds of opportunities and means of direct engagement in issues will help individual Disciples to become informed citizens who are good stewards of their political power. It will also help each congregation, each region, and the whole denomination become more faithful. As befits a people with a passion for justice, we Disciples should work *together* to create congregations that are truly alternative communities, that are safe places where all people are respected; where the moral ambiguity of life and our own participation in sin is acknowledged; where justice is viewed as an integral part of a deep Christian spirituality; where opportunities for public witness, action, and service are offered and nurtured; where people are helped to frame local and global issues in a context of Christian faith; where people learn about root causes of injustice and are supported in taking risks to do justice and to love kindness in the name of Christ; where people are empowered as agents of change in a postmodern world.

Churchwide Initiatives

A number of initiatives are underway within the Christian Church (Disciples of Christ) that have direct application and benefit for congregations as well as the whole church as we *all* seek to be faithful. These initiatives each seek to deepen and strengthen the integrity of our spirituality, community, and justice. It is my hope that individuals and congregations across the life of the Christian Church (Disciples of Christ) will participate in these initiatives.

Process of Discernment

The "process of discernment" is an approach that was originally developed in 1993 and is still being tested and strengthened. This approach was developed because it was observed by general church leadership and others that the old "debate and vote" approach, while still useful for some issues, is often not very helpful in moving the church toward faithfulness. Indeed, the "debate and vote" approach often leads to division, generating more heat than light. The process of discernment concept was developed as an alternative method for addressing important issues, especially those around which the church has no real consensus or common approach. A process of discernment may not seek to move the church toward a vote at all, but rather toward deep reflection and conversation until such time as it appears that a vote is appropriate or until there is an appropriate common course of action that becomes clear.

Two processes of discernment were begun as "pilots." As pilots, they had the right to succeed or to fail. The main point was to learn from them and to further develop the concept of processes of discernment.

The first pilot process of discernment was on a doctrinal issue: the authority of scripture. The steering committee was appointed and worked very hard at developing a way for the church to engage in discernment on this issue; however, it was concluded that the process of discernment model was not the best model for this particular issue because it was found that nearly *everyone* believes the Bible is authoritative, yet how this is manifest is evident only when there is conversation regarding particular issues. Thus, this process of discernment was discontinued and, in its place, a Commission on Faith and Understanding was developed. This model is described below.

The second pilot process of discernment is on racism in the church. The purpose of this process has not been to discern *whether* racism is wrong (we know the answer to that), but *how* racism manifests itself in our church's life and in our personal lives, and what we can do about it. This process of discernment has given rise to a churchwide anti-racism/pro-reconciliation initiative, which will be discussed below.

Thus, each of the two pilot processes of discernment have given birth to new models for nurturing true community, deep Christian spirituality, and a passion for justice within our life as a church. A third process of discernment was authorized by the General Assembly at Denver in 1997 on the "Participation of Gay and Lesbian Persons in the Life of the Church."

Anyone who reads the newspapers knows that homosexuality is an issue that has brought division to many denominations. This is one of those issues for which the old "debate and vote" method seems particularly ill-suited. Thus, we now have a process of discernment underway that seeks to incorporate what we learned from the two pilot processes. The point of this process of discernment is not to bring the church to a vote; rather, it is designed to be a resource to the whole church in congregations, regions, general units, and other institutions as each seeks to live faithfully in regard to questions such as who shall be ordained, who shall serve as pastor, who shall serve at the table, and other such questions as confront the church day-to-day in its various expressions. It is hoped that the process of discernment on "Participation of Gay and Lesbian Persons in the Life of the Church" will provide a model and will generate useful resources for the church as we all struggle with this important but often volatile issue.

I have no doubt that the future will bring other processes of discernment as the church struggles with other important and difficult questions.

The Anti-Racism/Pro-Reconciliation Initiative

The anti-racism/pro-reconciliation initiative grew out of the process of discernment on racism, one of the two original pilot processes of discernment. The anti-racism/pro-reconciliation initiative has been authorized by the General Board and is now being implemented by large numbers of regions, and by congregations within those regions, and by several general units. The aim is to see every congregation, region, general unit, and other institution of the church in the United States[2] implement this initiative over the next several years.

Of course, racism in the United States did not develop overnight. It has a five-hundred-year history. Thus, it will take some time for the church to come to grips with it and to become the kind of effective witness against racism that we would like to be. But this initiative has already changed us as a church in significant ways as we have examined ourselves and how we operate in our life together. More and more Disciples are coming to see "anti-racism" as a *positive* phrase rather than a negative phrase. Community, spirituality, and justice are all at stake in this issue. I believe the church's very soul and witness are at the

---

[2]In Canada the racial history is very different and so the congregations there will need a somewhat different approach than that which is currently being offered for U.S. congregations. Work is currently underway to develop an analysis of racism consistent with Canadian history.

2020 Vision for the Christian Church (Disciples of Christ)

heart of the matter. We will lack integrity so long as racism exists in our life as a church. Racism is sin.

The Commission on Faith and Understanding

If one were to draw a continuum of public witness methodologies, you could put sense of the assembly resolutions on one end of the continuum and processes of discernment on the other end. Sense of the assembly resolutions are debated for a matter of minutes in General Assembly and are then voted on. Churchwide processes of discernment take years to do well and are sometimes designed not to lead to a vote at all. Although each of these methodologies have their place, they are not always the best options. So we are developing some alternatives that fit somewhere between the sense of the assembly resolution and the process of discernment.

One expression of this effort is the "Commission On Faith and Understanding." This commission has sixteen members who represent the various parts of the church in terms of geography, race, ethnicity, gender, and age. It includes scholars, pastors, and lay members. The commission seeks to provide insight into issues when they are referred from the General Board, the General Assembly, or the General Minister and President. This is a model that I think is worthy of consideration for use in our congregations.

Unfortunately, not many of our congregations have a way of dealing creatively with complicated and controversial issues. Consequently, often only two options are utilized. One option is to do nothing about these issues, trying to keep the lid on, hoping they will go away. A passion for justice is destroyed by this sort of "avoidance" strategy. The other option is to engage in a knock-down, drag-out fight in which there are winners and losers. This is an option that tends to destroy true community. Neither of these two options serves to deepen Christian spirituality.

In the congregation, as in general and regional assemblies, there is a place for sense of the assembly resolutions and for processes of discernment. I believe there is also a place for a Commission on Faith Understanding (a congregation might use a different name for it). This would provide a place to actively engage the congregation in dialogue about an issue by providing a context of information that has biblical, theological, and moral content. The purpose would not be to make decisions for the congregation, but to provide a framework and to resource individuals and the congregation as a whole as they think and pray and dialogue about specific issues. The object is to move us from "posturing and positioning" based on mere emotional responses to the possibility of deeper conversation and prayer.

Who would serve on such a CFU in a congregation? Many congregations have educators who could take part. Certainly some spiritually mature elders should be a part. A wide range of ages should be included. Outside resource persons could be drawn in to consider specific issues. If there is a seminary nearby, a faculty member might be willing to help. Because most congregations with seminary trained pastors tend to under-utilize the pastor's seminary training, I think the pastor should also be a member.

Even if there are no immediate controversies underway or bubbling beneath the surface in a congregation, a CFU can work on longer-range issues such as resourcing a conversation about a changing neighborhood and how it affects the congregation's mission, or the congregation's policies in issues regarding human sexuality, or developing a study document on the role of elders.

The Bethany Project

The Bethany Project was developed in 1994 and was originally funded by the Lilly Endowment. It was originally designed to provide essential spiritual resources (including small groups for prayer and spiritual accountability) for pastors of congregations that are seeking to become revitalized. It continues to do this, but it has expanded its scope somewhat to include helping to strengthen the spiritual lives of people who are newly ordained or preparing for ordination through internships in "teaching" congregations where the leadership is effectively nurturing deep Christian spirituality, true community, and a passion for justice. While the Bethany Project is limited in scope and size (not everyone who might want to be a part of it can be accommodated), it serves as a reminder and an encouragement to every pastor to seek and to commit to a regimen of the spiritual disciplines that is lived out in accountability to a group of mature Christian leaders. Such a group can be developed by a local pastor where he or she is located. It may be composed entirely of Disciples or it may be ecumenical in scope of membership. Either way, it provides an important personal support and an accountability to the practice of the spiritual disciplines.

These are some of the churchwide initiatives being undertaken. I hope every reader understands that these churchwide initiatives are not meant to be implemented only in the general or regional life of the church. Each of these is intended ultimately to be a help to congregations seeking to be faithful. I hope that every reader, congregational pastor and lay leader alike, will think about how these initiatives can be applied and implemented or paralleled in your own congregation.

Growing

While one of the foremost temptations confronting the church today is the temptation to sacrifice quality in the name of quantity, a second is to sacrifice quantity in the name of quality. Or, more to the point, there is a temptation to use an *alleged* commitment to quality as an excuse to do nothing about quantity. I believe these are false dichotomies. It is not necessary to sacrifice quality for growth or vice versa. It is important for us to seek to be *both* a faithful *and* a growing church.

I want to state a fundamental conviction right here. *I believe God is calling the Christian Church (Disciples of Christ) to again become a growing church.*

I readily admit that such a statement could easily come simply out of my love for this church. After all, I was nurtured in it. I remember with joy and thankfulness being baptized at the age of ten by Wayne Drash at Mirror Lake Christian Church in St. Petersburg. I remember when my family and I became charter members of Palm Lake Christian Church, in which I was loved and encouraged. I felt a call to ministry that was nurtured by my pastors, Ken Dean, George Farmer, and J. W. Cate. There is a long list of Disciples saints who mentored and befriended me. It has been my privilege to serve some truly wonderful congregations, from very small to rather large. To be called by the church to regional and general ministry has certainly been affirming. Therefore, one might dismiss my conviction that this church should grow as a product of mere sentimentality. Not so.

Some might dismiss this conviction as counter to the Disciples' commitment to ecumenism. If we are truly ecumenical, does it really matter whether the Christian Church (Disciples of Christ) lives or dies? I believe it does matter. While the search for the visible unity of the whole church of Jesus Christ goes on, it is important that *every* church that effectively nurtures faith in Jesus Christ grows in faithfulness and in numbers. The numerical decline of the Christian Church (Disciples of Christ) does not further the vision of Christian unity!

In fact, if the Christian Church (Disciples of Christ) died for any reason other than an intentional blending into a more faithful and effective church, I believe God would want to reinvent it. I say this because, despite our shortcomings and failures, I believe we Disciples have an important witness to the world and make an important contribution to the whole body of Christ. Our particular way of being and doing church, our particular ethos, enriches the church universal. Our belief in Christian unity and keeping faith and reason connected are an important Disciples legacy—especially important in a postmodern world that is given to fragmentation and the common notion that one must choose between faith and reason.

I believe God is calling the Christian Church (Disciples of Christ) to again become a growing church because, at our best, we enrich the whole body of Christ and speak an important word to the postmodern world, and because our congregations have a tremendous impact. Have you ever stopped to think about the impact your particular congregation has on the world? Most of us have no idea how great this impact is.

Think for a moment about the number of people who have been baptized over the course of the life of your congregation. Think about the number of people who have been taught in Sunday school and other settings. Think of the number of persons who have been married and, yes, buried, and the number of friends and family members whose lives have been touched by your congregation's ministries during those important times of passage. Think of the people who have received advice and counsel, the people who received a helping hand at a moment of economic stress (some have been members of your congregation and some have been people who have had no affiliation with any church but who were helped in the name of the gospel). Think of how your congregation ministers to people who are present in worship only because they are with friends or family for a weekend. Think about the people whose lives are affected in this secular era by the mere presence of your building, which reminds people of God's presence. Think about the presence of your minister(s) and members in your town or city as they interact with others daily. Think about the mission work that is going on daily in your region, in your nation, and around the world because of the offerings that are sent out for work beyond your own congregation.

Whether your congregation is large or small, old or young, the number of people impacted over time in these ways and others is immense! Now, multiply the numbers of persons your congregation has touched by the thousands of congregations that compose the whole Christian Church (Disciples of Christ) and the numbers are stunning! Do we really believe that this impact, this influence in the world, is unimportant? On the contrary, I believe God wants this church, its ministry, and mission, to grow in faithfulness *and* numbers.

But we have *not* been growing in numbers as a communion. In fact, we have seen a remarkably steady decrease in numbers of members since 1968.

Figure 7-1: Total Membership of the Christian Church (Disciples of Christ) 1984–1998.

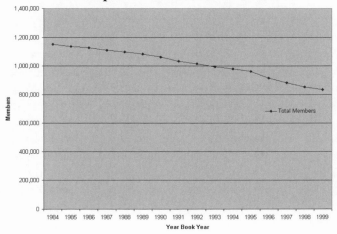

Note that between 1984 and 2000 we declined in total membership from 1,137,340 to 834,037. How did we lose these members? Certainly these losses reflect a shrinkage in the numbers of members of many individual congregations; however, many of these losses are also related to the death of significant numbers of Disciples congregations. Look at figure 7-2, a graph of the number of Disciples congregations between 1978 and 1998.

Figure 7-2: Numbers of Disciples Congregations, 1978–1998.

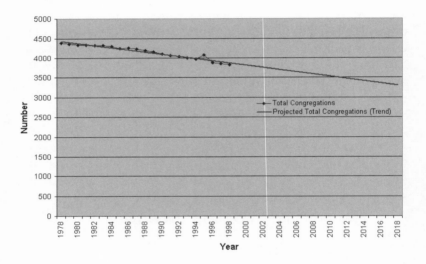

The fact is that congregations have life cycles, as do all institutions and every living thing. Some congregations live for many centuries (their maturation curves are long and often have many ups and downs from their beginning to their end); others are rather short lived (their maturation curves are relatively simple and brief). For most of our nearly two-hundred-year history we Disciples started more congregations than were dying. But from 1965 to 1980 we started almost no congregations. Finally, in the decade of the 1980s, we became intentional about new congregation establishment again and set a goal of one hundred new congregations, ten per year for ten years. We met this goal, but more than ten Disciples congregations die each year and several more leave the denomination each year for one reason or another ("leaving the denomination" is often a prelude to the death of a congregation as they cut themselves off from the resources and grounding of the wider church). Thus, statistically, our decline has two primary causes: the loss of membership in many existing congregations and the loss of congregations to death and other causes.

So how can this become a growing church again? (1) By our currently waning congregations' becoming revitalized and (2) by starting new congregations. I have attempted to point the way to revitalization. Congregations become revitalized (faithful and growing), in part, by focusing on mission rather than survival; by developing true community, a deep Christian spirituality, and a passion for justice; by identifying, enlisting, and nurturing leaders. These are some of the ways in which our congregations can become places of which unchurched people and seekers will want to become a part.

What about starting new congregations? Establishing *new* faithful and growing congregations is an essential strategy for reaching the unchurched. It is a matter of putting congregations where the unchurched live. This means starting congregations wherever there is significant growth in the number of residents (since World War II this has meant especially the growing suburbs of our cities). But putting congregations where the unchurched live also means starting congregations where there are not many congregations. This suggests that we should also be starting new congregations in the older urban centers of North America, from which many people left for the suburbs in recent decades, where new populations are moving in (including African Americans, Hispanics, and Asian Americans) and where there are often few viable congregations of any denomination.

The chart on the next page shows that we have been losing congregations to death and other causes at the rate of about forty-five congregations per year. In chapter 1 I said that there are three primary factors contributing to the shrinkage of the Christian Church (Disciples of Christ): the shift in North American culture, the survival mentality that has infected so many of our existing congregations in recent decades, and the small numbers of new congregations we have been starting since 1960. These three factors are interrelated, but the most concrete factor is the third: our failure to start new congregations at a significant rate. If we are going to grow in numbers, as I believe God is calling us to do, then we will have to both revitalize existing congregations and, especially, start new congregations that are vital and growing. How many congregations do we need to start in order to be a growing communion again?

Figure 7-3: Twenty Year Totals of Gains and Losses of Congregations

Gains	Losses
237 new	534 closed
18 reentered	295 withdrawn
5 mergers	29 mergers
	62 removed (per resolution 9516[3])
260 total gains	920 total losses

As we see in figure 7-3, based on the figures for the last twenty years of the twentieth century (1979–1999), we have been losing (for all reasons) about forty-five congregations per year. Thus, to stem our decline, we must start and sustain forty-five congregations per year; however, if we believe God calls us to *grow* and not merely to "hold our own," then we will need to start more than forty-five congregations per year. I believe a target of fifty per year is appropriate. Remembering that over the last twenty years we have been starting only about twelve congregations per year, we have our work cut out for us! We also know that new congregation establishment is a complicated undertaking, and we will not be able to jump from twelve new church starts per year to fifty per year immediately. But if we make new congregation establishment a priority for our life together now and begin increasing the number of congregations

---

[3]Resolution 9516 established a policy by which congregations that do not "report" for ten consecutive years are removed from the Yearbook. "Reporting" consists of returning the annual forms that are provided to each congregation by the Office of the Yearbook through regional church offices. These brief forms ask for basic information regarding membership, finances, and outreach and provide a way of measuring the health of our congregations.

we start each year, by 2020 we will have started the one thousand new congregations needed for us to be growing again in total numbers of congregations.

Actually, I believe that if we commit ourselves to at least one thousand new congregations between 2000 and 2020, we will actually see an *accelerated* rate of revitalization in our *existing* congregations due to the renewed sense of mission such an effort will engender. This accelerated revitalization of existing congregations could well mean fewer congregations dying and thus a numerical "turnaround" sooner than 2020. In any case, one thousand new Disciples congregations begun between 2000 and 2020, each seeking to realize true community, a deep Christian spirituality, and a passion for justice, would be a significant step forward in faithfulness and growth!

Diversity

I believe God is calling the Christian Church (Disciples of Christ) to greater racial and ethnic diversity.

Many of our regions, general units, and other institutions are already engaged in an anti-racism/pro-reconciliation initiative. The hope is that eventually every congregation and every other institution of the church will participate. Certainly a church that is committed to true community must seek to eliminate every vestige of racism from its own life, so that it may offer an anti-racist witness to the world at large.

In 2000, the Christian Church was composed of a member-ship that was approximately 93 percent European American. The other 7 percent includes Hispanic Disciples, Asian American Disciples, and African American Disciples. Of course, a much larger proportion of North Americans generally are of black, Hispanic, and Asian origins, and we must respond to all of those who live in our North American mission field. The fact that the Christian Church (Disciples of Christ) is currently predominantly European American is a reflection of our origins on the American frontier of the early 1800s; however, by increasing the proportion of our members who are African American, Hispanic, and Asian American, we will better reflect the changing realities of our primary mission field (North America). By 2020 it is anticipated that 14 percent of U.S. citizens will be African American, 17 percent will be Hispanic, and 6 percent will be Asian American. This means we will want to start a disproportionate number of new congregations in areas where these Americans live in order to begin to be a church that truly reflects the diversity of our mission field.[4]

All this means something of a change in the way we have been starting congregations. In the current model used to begin most European American congregations, a region provides a large amount of capital, which is typically used for the purchase of a site, some help with a first building, and support for a "pastor developer." One very large problem with this model is the fact that most regions spent all their new congregation establishment capital funds when we undertook the goal of one hundred new congregations in the 1980s. The pastor developer model often requires as much as a half million dollars from a region for each new congregation, and most regions simply do not have these kinds of funds.

Another problem lies in the fact that most regions already have as much as they can effectively do without adding the task of new congregation establishment. Consequently, regional new church committees are often hampered not only by a lack of capital funds but also by the slow pace at which regions are able to respond to needs. Many a prime site for a new congregation has been lost because the regional church "system" just couldn't respond quickly enough to make the needed purchase. I experienced this dynamic from three different perspectives: as founding pastor of a new congregation, as pastor of a congregation that was seeking to get a new congregation started by a region, and as a regional minister. The problem is not lack of interest on the part of regional ministers or regional committees. The problem is an overloaded system that cannot respond as quickly as needed.

This suggests to me that *congregations will have to be started more often by congregations, with the blessing and nurture of regions and with coordinating help from the general Office of New Congregation Establishment.* As I see it, the regions and the Office of New Congregation Establishment will keep the need for new

---

[4] Some of these congregations will be predominantly of one race or ethnicity. Others will be multicultural and multiracial in membership.

congregations before the whole church, encouraging existing congregations to commit to new congregation establishment; will identify target areas where new congregations should be established; will help identify and enlist potential new congregation pastors and lend whatever other expertise and support they have to offer; and give advice and counsel to new congregation establishment committees of existing congregations. In addition, the Office of New Congregation Establishment will need to provide a coordinating function that crosses regional boundaries.

When I say congregations will have to be started *by congregations*, I mean that most of the money, energy, and encouragement will need to come from individual congregations that have a vision for new congregations. In many cases this will mean a congregation starting a new congregation in another part of the same town or city. In other cases this will mean a congregation providing the resources to start a congregation somewhere else in their region or in another region that may be hundreds or thousands of miles away. I mention this latter possibility because new congregations are needed in places where there are no nearby Disciples congregations or none that are strong enough to engage in such a project, and because some Disciples congregations are in places that cannot support or do not need another new Disciples congregation. So, for example, a strong congregation in a small Oklahoma city might choose to provide the resources to start a new congregation in Los Angeles or Miami or New York City. Likewise, a predominantly European American congregation might choose to start an African American, Hispanic, Asian American, or multicultural/multiracial congregation.

Perhaps because of the survival mentality I mentioned before, many of our congregations think they are not capable of starting another congregation, though they well may be. Members of existing congregations tend to think, *We need all the resources we can gather to keep* this *congregation going*. Yet it is often when a congregation assumes a project that represents a real stretch for mission that they find their own ministry growing and thriving. We really *do* "find our life" in giving ourselves away for Christ's sake, even as Jesus said.

Some will argue that we should concentrate on filling the pews in the congregations we already have before we worry about starting new congregations. But it is just this kind of thinking that has resulted in our numerical decline in recent decades. It is not a matter of either-or, but of both-and: *both* revitalizing existing congregations *and* starting new ones. Most people who are not currently members will not drive more than a few miles to attend an existing congregation. They will tend to seek a congregation that is close to where they live, for the sake of convenience. This is why most new congregation experts say that no more than three miles is needed between congregations of the same denomination in a typical urban area.

Again, it is as a congregation (and the whole church) pours itself out in the mission of Jesus Christ that it finds its life.

Leadership Development

I believe God is calling the Christian Church (Disciples of Christ) to leadership development.

If existing congregations are going to be revitalized and to grow, and if new congregations are going to be established for European American, African American, Hispanic, and Asian American Disciples, then we are going to have to become committed to serious leadership development. We need more and better lay leaders; we need more and better licensed ministers; we need more and better ordained ministers.

Compared with twenty years ago, our ministers are retiring three years sooner on average. The good news is that this is partly because ministers can *afford* to retire these days thanks to the pension fund and to the fact that more congregations are compensating ministers more adequately. The bad news is that earlier retirement means ministers are actively serving three years less, which effectively shrinks the active ministry pool.

Compared with twenty years ago (when the trend toward "second career" ministries had already begun), active ministers are three years older on average. The good news is that second career people are bringing secular experience to their ministries. The bad news is that later starts, coupled with earlier retirements, make the average length of service much shorter.

In the early 1980s this church was ordaining about 120 people per year on average. By 2000 we were ordaining about ninety people per year on average. That is a decrease of 30 percent in just twenty years!

If we extend that twenty-year trend (1980–2000) to 2020, with the accelerating elements of fewer ordinations, earlier retirements, and later age of entry factored in, we can project a decrease in the active ministry pool from 3,347 in 1998 to approximately 1,650 in 2018. We can see the dramatic impact of these trends in the following illustration:

Figure 7-4: Number of Congregations Compared with Numbers of Ministers, 1978–2018.

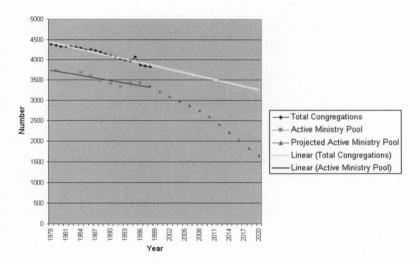

We can see from this chart that we have an inadequate supply of ministers even if we intend to continue shrinking. If we intend to grow, we will have to identify, enlist, and train significant numbers of ministers in the years ahead.

Another way to see the issue of ministerial supply is to look at the actual ages of ministers in the ministerial pool in 1998 (the latest data that was available).

In the chart on the next page we see that the great numbers of people who entered ministry after World War II have retired. Also, we see the significant number of people in their fifties who came into ministry during the Vietnam War era. Note that the number of persons in ministry drops off rather drastically after the Vietnam era. It is projected that a whopping 64 percent of all ministers currently in active service will retire by the year 2020!

Figure 7-5: 1998 Clergy Age Distribution.

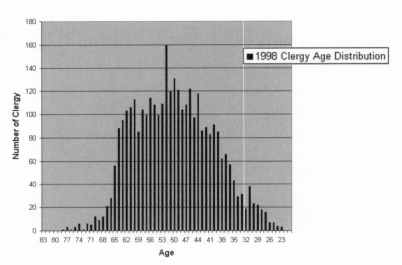

If we project the number of ministers needed to provide leadership at current levels into the year 2020 and compare that with the number actually projected, we find that by 2020 we will have a shortfall of ministers of approximately 1,250 (see figure 7-6).

Thus, in order to maintain the current proportion of ministers to congregations, we will need to ordain (or recognize the ordinations of persons coming to the Disciples from other traditions) or license ministers at the rate of an additional eighty to ninety per year. If we are going to start one thousand new congregations, we will need to ordain or license a total of about 230 per year. It is abundantly clear that we must be about identifying, enlisting, and educating people for ministry!

Identification and enlistment for ministry requires a thoroughgoing partnership between congregations, regions, general units, colleges, and seminaries. The leadership of all these partner institutions must be constantly looking for potential candidates for ministry, seeking those who have gifts and graces for ministry from among the brightest and best. Who in your congregation, whether youth or adult, might be a candidate for ministry? Who in that week of camp and conference should be encouraged to think about ministry?

Figure 7-6: Projected Ministerial Supply

Year	Needed to maintain current cong./minister ratio	Current Projection	Difference
2000	3,300	3,225	75
2002	3,255	3,100	155
2004	3,210	2,990	320
2006	3,165	2,850	315
2008	3,120	2,750	370
2010	3,075	2,600	475
2012	3,030	2,450	580
2014	2,985	2,225	760
2016	2,940	2,000	940
2018	2,895	1,800	1,095
2020	2,850	1,600	1,250

The Christian Church (Disciples of Christ) has many small congregations (as do most all denominations).

Figure 7-7: Congregations by Size of Worship Attendance in 1998.

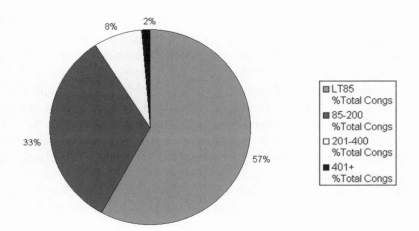

Note that 57 percent of our congregations have fewer than eighty-five persons attending worship on average, and, if present trends continue (that is, if no revitalization occurs), that proportion is projected to increase to nearly 77 percent of currently existing congregations by 2020 (figure 7-8).

Figure 7-8: Congregations by Projected Size of Worship Attendance in 2020.

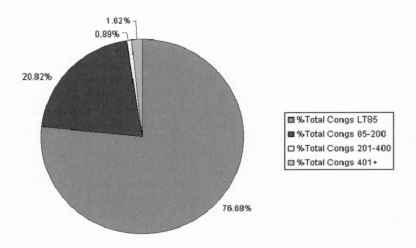

This is significant because most congregations with fewer than eighty-five in worship cannot afford a full-time minister. Thus, most of these congregations will need to be served by lay ministers or bivocational ministers. This means that many more candidates for licensed and bivocational ministry will need to be identified, enlisted, trained, and nurtured.

Although some of our seminaries have begun experimenting with programs for the training of licensed ministers, most are overwhelmingly focused on ordained ministry. Without diminishing the focus on ordained ministry (since we will need more ordained ministers as well for the revitalization of existing congregations and the starting of new congregations), we need our seminaries to establish an effective program for licensed ministers as well. The new distance-learning methodologies will be an important component of such programs, since most persons preparing for, and enhancing their skills for, licensed ministry cannot spend much time on a seminary campus. Such distance-learning methodologies will also play an increasing role in continuing education for those already ordained and licensed.

I believe our seminaries will also have an increasing role in the continuing education of lay leadership. Of course, through the preparation of ordained ministers, seminaries have always contributed to the education of laypeople (at least to the degree that our ministers have engaged in teaching laypeople, which I believe is a terribly important role for pastors). But I believe we also need seminaries to become involved directly in the provision of teaching materials and media for laypeople. This is because, in the face of the information age and a world of competing religious and philosophical notions, laypeople (especially lay leaders) can no longer be satisfied with merely popular, shallow perspectives on Christian faith. There is too much to know for laypeople to be satisfied or adequately fed with secondhand information and "do-it-yourself" Christian education.

I have focused here on seminaries, but their work must be done in partnership with pastors, with regions, and with general units of the church. Gone is the time when leadership develop-ment could be compartmentalized into the work of one organi-zation, unit, or institution of the church. All our church's institutions must get beyond traditional territorial thinking and become partners with one another in providing what the church needs for its congregations, its ministers, and its lay leadership.

Seeing with 2020 Vision

So, what is God calling us to be and do as we move toward 2020?

I SEE A CHURCH that manifests true community, a deep Christian spirituality, and a passion for justice. From the Old Testament and the New, from the prophet Micah to Jesus' teaching of the Great Commandment, I believe God is calling us to become this kind of church.

I SEE A CHURCH that looks a lot like what *The Design* of the Christian Church (Disciples of Christ) describes. We restructured ourselves in 1968 on the basis of covenant. I believe we still need to develop our understanding of covenant and the realization of a covenant community. We need to move from what often looks like a culture of autonomy to a culture *of dependence on God's Spirit and interdependence with each other.*

We must enter the future God has for us *together.* This new world is not one in which single, isolated, independent congregations are going to do well. Such congregations may look at the moment as though they are thriving, but the cultural undertow of secularism is so great that such isolated communities of faith are inevitably going to be dragged under by the currents to drown and die, or worse, to become purveyors of a sectarian religion that is in cahoots with the principalities and powers rather than confronting them and helping God convert them. This is not about the survival of the denomination; it is about standing together in order to be faithful to our mission in a culture that is often hostile to Christian faith. We must help our members understand the importance of being a part of the Christian Church (Disciples of Christ) and to understand and live out our covenant as one communion within the larger community of the whole of the church of Jesus Christ.

I SEE A CHURCH that is clear about the gospel: that God was in Christ reconciling the world to himself, not counting their trespasses against them, and entrusting the message of reconciliation to us.

I SEE A CHURCH that is clear about what it means to be the church: not a club or a mere social organization, but the body of Christ.

I SEE A CHURCH that is faithful to its mission "to be and to share the good news of Jesus Christ, witnessing and serving from our doorsteps to the ends of the earth."

I SEE A CHURCH that is less focused on survival and has developed a passion for mission.

I SEE A CHURCH that faithfully and effectively addresses the postmodern world, effectively teaching children and youth, and that has begun reaching Generation Xers in significant numbers.

I SEE A CHURCH that understands that, as important as overseas ministries are (and they are very important), North America is our primary mission field, a church whose congregations regard themselves as mission stations.

I SEE A CHURCH whose ministers have moved the focus of their ministry from management to modeling relationship with

God, a church whose ministers are giving authentic Disciples spiritual leadership and who are not burned out or depressed but who are energized, joy filled, and Spirit led.

I SEE A CHURCH that values diversity, welcomes difference, and embraces unity as a sign of God's love for all peoples and cultures and that has recaptured its commitment to the unity of all Christians as a sign and a foretaste of God's good news to a broken and hostile world.

I SEE A CHURCH that has faced up to its bigotry and racism and has begun to live its justice pronouncements with integrity.

I see a church with no gaps of trust between the membership and the leadership.

I SEE A CHURCH that takes worship seriously.

I SEE A CHURCH whose general and regional assemblies reinforce our sense of family, resource our congregations' life and mission, and give us joyous encouragement as we worship God together.

I SEE A CHURCH in which we engage in serious biblical, theological, and moral discernment, acting boldly and faithfully on what we discern while maintaining the unity of the Spirit in the bond of peace.

I SEE A CHURCH in which our leadership is forging vibrant new covenantal partnerships across old rigid bureaucratic boundaries that have tied us down and kept us focused on our past rather than on God's possibilities for our future.

And, yes, I SEE A CHURCH that is growing spiritually and numerically.

I believe we are exactly the kind of church people of this generation are looking for! No leader today knows *exactly* what the future holds or *exactly* how God will get us to it. But I believe we have enough clarity to understand that God has an important place for us in the new world, in the new millennium, and that we will get there if we move with faithfulness and commitment.

May God bless us each as we seek to be this kind of faithful, growing church for 2020 and beyond.

APPENDIX 1

Why Bother with Denominations?

Members tend to think of their congregation as being simply a local phenomenon. Unless we intentionally think about it, we unconsciously assume that the congregation of which we are a member just sprang up where it is entirely by the efforts of the people who live (or who lived) near where the congregation is located. The fact is, however, that almost every one of our nearly 4,000 congregations was first imagined, and was intentionally established, by people who did not live in the neighborhood.

Nearly every one of our congregations was born of and into a church family called the Disciples of Christ. Being born into this particular family (or, in the case of congregations that began in another tradition, being adopted into this particular family) has shaped the identity and ways of being and doing of each. If we do not understand this faith family that birthed and launched our congregation (or that at the very least has nurtured it), we will not understand why we are the way we are, with our strengths and weaknesses and propensities; we will not understand how change can be most effectively accomplished in our congregation.

Elton Trueblood was right in speaking of people today as a "cut flower civilization." A cut flower civilization, as Trueblood uses the metaphor, is one that is cut off from its roots, one that has no means by which to draw nurture and sustenance from its soil. This painfully describes all of us who live in this secular era of "future shock," of lightning-paced change. Because of the geographic and socioeconomic mobility typical of so many of us today, we feel cut off from our origins (or have *deliberately* cut ourselves off from our origins), from that which launched us in life. This tendency is also evident in the realm of current congregational life, as many local leaders assume that denominational connection is "obsolete and unimportant" or even a liability. While there are certainly problems, challenges and obsolete structures and approaches in denominations today, just as there are in congregations, denominations remain an important factor in congregational life and health. Therefore, we Disciples need to take the time to think about who we are as a faith family called the "Disciples of Christ."

I use the word "denomination" to describe the *institution* we call the Christian Church (Disciples of Christ). It is an institution that holds together as one body some four thousand institutions called congregations, thirty-five institutions called regions, eleven institutions called general units, and a host of other institutions within these institutions. But the Christian Church (Disciples of Christ) in the United States and Canada is more than just an "institution of institutions." It has a *spiritual and theological reality* that transcends mere institutional reality just as a person is more than a collection of bones, muscles, and organs. We are nothing less than a part of the whole body of Jesus Christ, the church universal. Thus, when we speak of our "denomination," we are speaking in very limited ways. A more spiritually and theologically complete way of describing the Christian Church (Disciples of Christ) in the United States and Canada is to speak of it as a *communion.*

> Indeed, the body does not consist of one member but of many…The eye cannot say to the hand, "I have no need of you," nor again the head to the feet, "I have no need of you"…If one member suffers, all suffer together with it; if one member is honored, all rejoice together with it. (1 Cor. 12:14, 21, 26)

One of the things I learned in parish ministry is that most members do not care much about the denomination of which they are a part. They choose a congregation with which they feel comfortable without very much thought about the communion of which it is a part. In regard to denominational "stuff," at best they assume that it is more or less necessary and being done reasonably competently by someone who is trustworthy, and that they can thus ignore it. At worst they see giving to Basic Mission Finance[1] as something like making franchise payments! This attitude is not unique to the church.

I very much enjoyed being a member of the Rotary Club for eight years; however, I seldom thought about Rotary International. Our club's members knew the larger organization was necessary and even that "they" did good things, but "they" remained a "they" for the most part. We were glad someone else was taking care of "it," but most of us did not want to think about much beyond our local club. I remember how we would inwardly groan when it was announced it was time for the annual visit from the district governor. The annually elected district governors were sometimes poor public speakers, and their mostly ceremonial appearances interrupted the flow of what we were doing in our local club. Nevertheless, we grudgingly admitted that we needed to be responsible members of the larger organization, and so most of us dutifully turned out for a governor's visit as an act of club loyalty.

A few years later, when I was a regional minister visiting congregations, I sometimes felt like a visiting "district governor." I used to joke that my goal in these visits was to preach so effectively that the second time I visited there would be a normal attendance. Most members just do not get very excited when they hear a regional or general church leader is coming to their congregation. This is a pity, because these leaders of the wider church are most often fine Christians with an important witness and ministry. But most members of most congregations have little enthusiasm for the church beyond their congregation. This is partly a reflection of the times and partly a reflection of our failure to teach our members about the wider church. It is also a reflection of our failure to understand that, in a very real sense, the church is not just another organization but is an "organism"— the very *body* of Jesus Christ.

---

[1] Basic Mission Finance is our common global mission fund. Each Disciples congregation contributes a locally determined amount to this fund each year. In addition, in most congregations, individuals (through special day offerings) and Christian Women's Fellowship and other local groups contribute amounts. Churchwide, each year approximately twenty million dollars is given to Basic Mission Finance to support the work of the church beyond the congregation, including the ministry of regions, general units, institutions of higher education, and overseas mission.

I remember very well an occasion several years ago when I was in a meeting of people who were unhappy with some of the decisions taken at a previous General Assembly of the Christian Church (Disciples of Christ), the biennial gathering of some eight thousand congregational representatives from across the life of our church. After more than an hour of heated discussion, one person blurted out the question, "Why bother with denominations anyway?"

Of course, the question was being asked by a frustrated, disgruntled member. But I realized in that moment that this question crosses the mind of even relatively supportive members from time to time. Why bother with denominations anyway?

It's easy to see how such a question arises. After all, we could all think of local uses for that percentage of our congregation's budget that is sent to Basic Mission Finance. And during my years as a local pastor, I got as tired as anyone of traveling to this and that regional or general meeting. I do not always agree with the General Assembly myself! Some have even said that denominations are dying anyway, so what's the point? Why bother?

There are good answers to this question, as we shall see. But we can no longer take it for granted (and never really could) that individual Disciples know and appreciate why they and their congregations need to stay connected to the rest of the body. The cultural climate today is such that radical individualism and localism pervade the whole of North American culture and the mindset of North American churchgoers. Thus, people naturally tend to be disinterested in wider institutional life.

For example, I belong to the Athletic Club in downtown Indianapolis. It is a century-old institution. On the walls of the lobby, one sees pictures of club meetings that occurred sixty years ago. What strikes one about these old pictures is the fact that the attending members filled the meeting room—*several hundred* members were present. The Athletic Club has about the same number of participating members today; however, if the club called a general meeting for next week, unless there was some business that was "life or death" for the institution, the leadership would be hard pressed to get more than a couple of dozen members to show up. Today, people become members of the Athletic Club in order to have a place to exercise, to participate in sports, to take clients for a nice meal, and so forth, but not to be part of an institution. Even in our congregations, we find that we have to schedule congregational meetings at the close of worship before everyone scatters or in conjunction with a fellowship dinner if we want to have more than a handful of people hear the reports, elect officers, and so forth. These days people most often join a congregation to get their own perceived individual needs met, not to be part of an institution, even when that institution is an expression of the body of Christ.

The current cultural climate of radical individualism and localism causes members to think of their own congregation as being a freestanding entity that birthed itself and that has no particular need to be part of the larger body called the Christian Church (Disciples of Christ).

Even in the Roman Catholic Church, in which members assume and affirm the importance of local connection to a larger body, this radical individualism and localism are today chief determinants of individual Christian thought and behavior. For example, "Rome" can say what it will about what constitutes appropriate forms and uses of birth control, but individual North American Catholics are increasingly exercising their own judgment in such matters in numbers unimaginable fifty years ago. Individual Catholics do this even as they affirm that they belong to and respect the larger Roman Catholic Church. Whether one thinks this is good or bad, the point is that church people tend to think locally and individually these days.

The Christian Church (Disciples of Christ) was born in resistance to the excesses of nineteenth-century denominational power and control, and thus such individualism and localism come naturally to Disciples. So I think a case must be made for us Disciples as to why it is important for congregations to be part of a larger entity called "denomination." Otherwise, some readers will be tempted to look for the renewal (or transformation) of their congregation apart from the larger body of which they are a part, or as if they were not a part of a larger body.

As I see it, there are three primary functions of a denomination. The first is to make it possible to do *together* those parts of the mission that we cannot effectively do as individual congregations. The second is to nurture and sustain what I like to call an *ethos*, a particular way of doing and being "church." The third is to provide for accountability. I want to explore each of these a bit.

Doing Things Together

Clearly, the gospel of Jesus Christ is not merely a *local* gospel, and it is not just about individuals. Jesus commanded us to "go into all the world." In the book of Acts (1:8) Jesus speaks of us being his witnesses "in Jerusalem, in all Judea and Samaria, *and to the ends of the earth.*" The Mission Imperative Statement[2] of the Christian Church (Disciples of Christ) uses this language from Acts to describe the mission of the church: "to be and to share the Good News of Jesus Christ, witnessing, loving, and serving from our doorsteps '*to the ends of the earth.*'" Clearly, the mission of the church is a *global* mission. Yet what congregation can, by itself, be truly global in its outreach? Thus, we must work together in a way that goes beyond single congregations and national boundaries.

For example, congregations work together as denomination to accomplish overseas ministries. We work together as denomination to provide camp and conference programs for our children and youth. We work together to be heard in society on important social issues and to minister to the needs of the elderly, the young, and the differently abled. We work together to provide colleges and seminaries. We work together to provide effective programming for children and youth, including camp and conference. We work together to do leadership training and to provide opportunities for spiritual growth. We work together to provide congregations with a host of services that strengthen them for their mission, including publishing, consultation in the areas of architecture and financial campaigns, management of accumulated resources, education for stewardship, and leadership development. Congregations work together to call effective and responsible pastoral leadership and to support that leadership

---

[2]The Mission Imperative Statement was created by the General Board and the General Assembly in 1995 to help give focus to our work together. The Mission Imperative Statement is found on pages 4–5.

with provisions for pensions and health insurance that can follow ministers as they move all over North America. We work together to connect and share in mission with Christians of other denominations through ecumenical bodies. Most of us easily see the advantage of working together as denomination for these kinds of purposes.

Nurturing an Ethos

"Ethos" refers to the way we do things: how we worship, how we govern ourselves, what we think is most important and what we think is unimportant, how we decorate and do not decorate our buildings, what we call things, our characteristic attitudes. In short, our ethos is *who we are as a church family expressed in how we do things and how we think about things.* Now, at the outset I must say that no real Disciple would ever say, "Our Disciples ways of doing things are the *only* ways to do things if one is to be saved!" In fact, refusing to make such a claim is one of our Disciples ways. Our Disciples ways of doing things are not ultimate for us; God as revealed in Jesus Christ is ultimate. Nevertheless, we do have our preferred ways, and these ways of doing things mesh in a way that creates a more or less consistent and helpful pattern.

"Ethos" does not exist in churches only; for example, each family has its own ethos. I will use my own family as an example. When I married my wife, Mindy, I married into the Fishbaugh family, and I discovered they did many things differently from the Hamms. For example, when I was growing up, Christmas morning went like this: The first kid out of bed woke everyone else up (usually before 6 a.m.), my brother and I distributed the packages quickly, we ripped off the wrapping paper (at least my brother and I did), and by 7:30 all the packages were open and I was out comparing notes with my friends.

It is done differently in the Fishbaugh household.

At the Fishbaughs' you sleep in, then you get up for a leisurely breakfast or brunch, then you mosey into the front room and admire the tree and the gifts (many of which have appeared in the night). Pictures are taken, posed in front of the tree. By 10:30 a.m. or so it is time to open the gifts. Usually, only one package is opened at a time while the others watch and comment. The wrapping paper is rolled up and saved from year to year! By 1:00 p.m. or so we are finished.

My first Christmas with the Fishbaughs was quite a culture shock! The Fishbaugh Christmas "ethos" was considerably different than the Hamms's! It took me quite a while to appreciate the "Fishbaugh Christmas." But in time I came to appreciate the fact that some of the wrapping paper and boxes went back twenty years or more, and I found myself appreciating each gift more than I had under the "Hamm Christmas" regimen.

Was one way of doing Christmas "better" than the other? Well, I do not think anyone's salvation depends on doing it one way or the other! I learned to do it the Fishbaugh way because that's where Mindy and I went for Christmas (before children). Thanksgiving, on the other hand, is spent at my family's annual reunion, and so Mindy observes Thanksgiving according to the ways of *my* family of origin.

One thing I know: In our home today, Mindy and I and our children do Christmas according to the *Fishbaugh* ethos.

The point here is not that one way or the other is "better" in any *ultimate* sense. The point is that when, for example, a Brown marries into the Smith family, the Brown had better learn and do at least the important parts of the Smith family's ethos or there is going to be trouble! If I went to the Fishbaughs' house, arose on Christmas morning, and woke everybody up at 6:00, demanding that they come in and "do Christmas," I *guarantee* there would be trouble!

Likewise, being Disciples of Christ is not better in any ultimate sense than being Methodist or Presbyterian or Roman Catholic: Salvation comes through grace by faith, not by denominational affiliation.[3] But each of these traditions has its own ways of doing things, and we have to express ourselves as church by *some* consistent ethos or our church life will be chaotic, confused, and conflicted. If we are going to be Disciples of Christ, then we should know, understand, and appreciate the Disciples ethos.

---

[3]The fact that this understanding is today shared by most denominations represents a significant change from the days of the early nineteenth century, when the Disciples of Christ began. As a Christian unity movement, the Disciples have contributed, and continue to contribute, to this change.

That ethos is something that is much broader than the practices of one congregation. This is why when Disciples from one congregation visit a Disciples congregation somewhere else, they usually feel pretty much at home. It "fits" because they find generally the same ethos being practiced. While, for example, the particulars of how the Lord's supper is observed may differ somewhat from Disciples congregation to Disciples congregation, one can always depend on receiving communion in *any* Disciples congregation on *any* Sunday *anywhere*. While the style of worship may differ significantly from congregation to congregation, the worship service will involve laypeople in significant ways, and only a simple confession of faith is required of new members: "Do you believe that Jesus is the Christ and do you accept him as your Savior?"

Frankly, one of our problems as a denomination is that we often do a poor job of teaching new members who we are and what our ethos is. This is one reason we often see conflict in so many of our congregations. Sometimes, well-intentioned people come into the Disciples from other traditions without learning what our ethos is. They then begin acting like an insensitive Hamm at a Fishbaugh Christmas! Despite what may be their good intentions, trouble ensues because their actions and attitudes are not congruent with the Disciples ethos. Sometimes they draw a number of other members to their side because these other members do not know and understand the Disciples either; then there are not just one or two unhappy members, there is a full-blown church split.

Sadly, it is sometimes ministers who do not understand or who disregard the Disciples ethos. Congregational search committees are well advised to be certain that anyone they are considering to be pastor of their congregation knows, understands, and *appreciates* the Disciples ethos.[4]

---

[4]This is not an argument for rejecting all change that may be initiated by a pastor or other church leader. Rather, I mean that pastors and other leaders should give leadership that understands, appreciates, and is congruent with the Disciples of Christ ethos. This does not mean that such pastors and leaders will necessarily have grown up in this communion—they may be very new Disciples. But it does mean they will be helped to become familiar with our ethos before being invited to serve as primary leaders.

It is important for congregations to teach who we are as a church. This ethos is bigger than the particularities of any one congregation. It is a tradition widely shared by some 4,000 congregations. It is not a "lockstep" kind of tradition that requires uniformity. Each individual congregation has its own particularities (and peculiarities). Theologically, some congregations are conservative, some are moderate, and some are liberal. Some worship in an informal tradition, some in a more formal tradition. But in every congregation there are commonalities shared with the rest of the denomination that are always recognizable. For example, our congregations function democratically, and ministers and laypeople are of equal importance in leadership.

It is the responsibility of all our congregations individually and together as a denomination to teach and nurture this ethos, even as we recognize it is a "living" tradition and that ongoing appropriate change is desirable and inevitable. As Disciples we have the freedom to draw on the totality of Christian experience (Protestant, Roman Catholic, Orthodox, Pentecostal) to discover fresh, creative, and faithful ways of doing things. But we must be sure to incorporate these ways into our life carefully and sensitively in the light of our own ethos and with respect for the fullness of the traditions out of which these other ways of doing things come.

Providing for Accountability

Each of us needs accountability to someone. Our congregations and the other institutions and structures of our denomination need accountability also. This churchwide accountability to one another is one of the characteristics that sets us Disciples apart from nondenominational groups. While we Disciples enjoy tremendous freedom as individuals and as congregations, we also see ourselves as being in *covenant* with each other as well as with God. "Covenant" is a powerful biblical word found in both the Old and New Testaments. It does not imply a legalistic kind of accountability in which we have to have each other's *permission* to do this or that. Rather, covenant means we affirm that we have a kind of moral and spiritual accountability to each other in which we consider the good of the whole and consult with Disciples partners beyond our selves and our immediate group as we make our individual and collective decisions.

The ordination and licensing of ministers provides an example. Every region[5] of the Christian Church (Disciples of Christ) has a commission on ministry, which is made up of representatives from a variety of congregations around the region. A commission is typically composed of ten or twelve persons reflecting the region's membership: lay and ordained, male and female, younger and older, racially and culturally diverse, and so forth. These commissions typically meet regularly to nurture people who are preparing for ordained or licensed ministry. It is also the responsibility of these commissions to certify that these people are qualified and morally fit to do ministry in the name of the whole Christian Church (Disciples of Christ) and, therefore, to be licensed or ordained.[6] These two functions are often referred to as "nurture and certification."

When I was regional minister of Tennessee, a man came before our commission on ministry to seek licensing. He came to us from a nondenominational background. *Nondenominational* sounds like such an attractive word to us free-spirited North Americans, but what it most often really means is *unconnected and unaccountable to anyone beyond a congregation.* When he was questioned about his commitment to the Christian Church (Disciples of Christ), it became apparent that he had no denominational loyalties whatsoever. As he put it, "I am accountable only to Jesus Christ."

Well, yes. Ultimately, we are *all* accountable to Jesus Christ. But as we tried to help him see, very few of us are always capable of completely understanding Christ's will in every situation. Our own agendas enter into the picture, our own prejudices, and so we often do not recognize or discern what it is Christ would have us do. Sometimes we incorrectly identify our *own* strong desires and opinions as those of Jesus Christ. This is just part of being human, and so we have to have someone beyond ourselves to help keep us "honest" with ourselves and with Jesus Christ. Thus, we Disciples look to our denomination as a source of

---

[5]There are thirty-five regions in the United States and Canada.

[6]Or, if already ordained, to continue to have standing as a Disciples minister.

insight and for reality checks. Of course, the denomination does not always have the right answers, but the point is that the denomination does help us keep the right questions before us. In this case, it is a regional commission on ministry that asks the right questions to be sure that an individual seeking licensing or ordination is not inappropriately assuming that his or her opinions are divine and that he or she sees in anything other than a "mirror, dimly" (1 Cor. 13:12).

Ultimately, in regard to accountability, it is not even terribly important that the denomination be the Disciples of Christ. It could be United Presbyterian, or African Methodist Episcopal, or Greek Orthodox, or a host of other families of Christians. The point is, we need to be personally and systematically responsible to *someone* beyond ourselves, beyond even our own congregation—someone who can help us be accountable to Jesus Christ.

My point here is clearly, if tragically, illustrated by the controversy surrounding the televangelist Jimmy Swaggert. A few years ago, Swaggert was exposed as having frequented prostitutes. He confessed to his congregation, but he refused to accept the discipline of the denomination to which he belonged, the Assemblies of God, so the denomination removed his standing as a minister of the Assemblies of God. But his *congregation*, evidently so taken by his personality and apparent sincerity, said in effect, Fine, we'll leave the denomination, too, and be the church by ourselves. Who needs 'em? (In this case, the question was, Why bother with the Assemblies of God?)

Well, not long after, what every Disciples regional minister could have predicted would happen in fact happened. Swaggert was caught again with a prostitute. At first, Swaggert thought he was in serious jeopardy, so he made a public statement through his son that he was going to step down from his ministry and get counseling so that he could continue his ministry later. But then, "in prayer," as he put it, the Lord told him to continue his ministry and that "it was nobody else's business."

This kind of spiritual blindness, this outrageous self-service, is what often results when individuals, or even congregations, regions, general units, or other organizations within the life of the church think that they can always be their own inerrant interpreter of the will of Christ and of their own motives and actions. Any of us can be blinded by sin at times.

To our brother who was seeking licensing from the Christian Church in Tennessee, I finally posed the question this way: "Are you, or are you not, willing to submit yourself to the spiritual discipline of being a part of a denominational family?" He said he would think it over. So far as I know, he is still thinking it over, but it is unlikely that he will ever be licensed by a Disciples region anywhere until he finds the humility to admit the need we all have: the need for some concrete, systematic accountability. The idea that we can be Christians all by ourselves, without any connection to a larger part of the body of Christ, is a very seductive notion in this culture of individualism and "do your own thing." But it is a notion that *any* careful reading of scripture and human history will show to be disastrous and idolatrous.

As Protestants, we speak of "the priesthood of all believers." But many of us do not understand what the priesthood of all believers means. It does *not* mean "You be your own priest and I will be my own priest." What the priesthood of all believers *does* mean is "I will be your priest and you will be mine." It means we do not have to have any one particular person in one particular office to fill the role of priest. But *somebody* besides we ourselves must fill that role for us. We cannot be the church by ourselves. Others must represent (*mediate*, if you will) grace for us. Likewise, others must help us be accountable.

This is why Christ has established his church in congregations. As congregations, we are groups of Christians who mediate grace for one another and who call each other to accountability. But even congregations, even large congregations, are not able to stand by themselves in this regard. Groupings of congregations, most often called *denominations*, are also necessary.

Now, I will admit that it may sound pretty peculiar for a "Campbellite"[7] like me to argue for the necessity of denominations. After all, Campbell, Stone and the rest of our

---

[7]Disciples of Christ used to be called "Campbellites" by some because Thomas and Alexander Campbell were among our founders. Disciples did not like to be called Campbellites because it suggested the same kind of division in church life, based on human viewpoints, that they were seeking to overcome. Nevertheless, it was a common term in the nineteenth century.

forebears struggled with the denominationalism of their day and sought to bring about the unity of the church. But they were not really trying to eradicate denominations, nor were they seeking to make congregations autonomous. They were reacting to the narrow and exclusive claims and practices of particular denominations in their day. And as a Disciple today, *I* certainly react negatively to any denomination claiming that it is the only, or even the best, way to come to Christ.

Thomas and Alexander Campbell's idea was that if they could transform the church by using only New Testament forms and practices, the church would be free to come back together, freed from the human innovations that had divided it—human innovations such as creeds used as "tests of fellowship."[8] As our ecumenical officer Robert Welsh likes to say, "The Disciples are a denomination to end all denominations!"

But there is something about the church in the New Testament that Campbell and his colleagues seem not to have fully appreciated. Most of what we know about the church of the first century A.D. is found in Paul's letters. And what does a careful reading of Paul's letters reveal? Most of the letters were written in attempts to solve problems of discipline and accountability that were springing up in those young congregations. As Campbell soon came to see, the key to Christian unity was not to eliminate denominational structures, for *some* form of structure beyond the congregation is necessary. The key to Christian unity is to focus on the *spiritual* and theological reality of our oneness in Jesus Christ, so that the structures we create to govern our life as churches, and the doctrine we create to interpret the faith, will reflect our essential, God-given oneness in Christ.

In spite of tragic divisions within the Stone-Campbell movement, we Disciples of Christ should be proud of our heritage, which envisions a church united on the basis of the Spirit of the Living Christ rather than simply on the basis of New Testament

---

[8]The historic creeds of the church of Jesus Christ can be helpful and instructive when used as affirmations of faith. They can even be helpful as tools of clarification and accountability. However, using them as "tests of fellowship" means setting up these humanly created statements as absolute definitions of who is a Christian and who is not. The Disciples of Christ have always preferred a simple confession of faith that "Jesus is the Christ," rather than requiring assent to particular creeds.

forms. This vision has borne fruit in a profound way. For example, Christians of most denominations today recognize that salvation is not based on denominational affiliation or on particular doctrine, but on the "apostolic faith"[9] that "in Christ God was reconciling the world to himself, not counting their trespasses against them, and entrusting the message of reconciliation to us" (2 Cor. 5:19). In fact, the whole church of Jesus Christ of the past century has been blessed and strengthened in no small measure by this witness of the Disciples of Christ.

Our great gift to the wider church has perhaps been our understanding of Paul's letter to the church at Ephesus (4:4–6):

> There is one body and one Spirit [regardless of the fact that there are many styles of worship and forms of church government], just as you were called to the one hope of your calling, one Lord, one faith [many differing *beliefs* to be sure, but one *faith*], one baptism [differing *forms* of baptism, but only one *baptism*], one God and Father of us all, who is above all and through all and in all.

Paul goes on to say in verses 11–16,

> The gifts [God] gave were that some should be apostles, some prophets, some evangelists, some pastors and teachers, to equip the saints for the work of ministry, for building up the body of Christ, until all of us come to the unity of the faith [notice that Paul does not speak of a unity of *belief* but of a unity of *faith*] and of the knowledge of the Son of God, to maturity, to the measure of the full stature of Christ. We must no longer be children, tossed to and fro and blown about by every wind of doctrine…But speaking the truth in love, we must grow up in every way into him who is the head, into Christ, from whom the whole body, joined and knit together by every ligament with which it is equipped, as each part is working properly, promotes the body's growth in building itself up in love.

---

[9]The "apostolic faith" is simply a reference to the faith that was passed on to the church by the apostles of Jesus. This faith is perhaps most simply captured in Paul's statement here in 2 Corinthians 5:19.

No one can be the body of Christ by himself or herself. No one is an island. No congregation is an island. No denomination, even, is an island. We are each a part, and only a part, of the whole body of Christ. Each part needs every other part, because it is the very essence of the church God called into being and because we need the other parts to keep us honest. We are accountable to Christ through his *whole* body, through the *whole* church. Denominations, then, provide a matrix of accountability that holds all the individuals and all the institutions within the church accountable to each other.

So why bother with denominations? For the sake of doing things together, for nurturing an ethos, and for mutual accountability.

Frankly, I believe denominations are really just temporary structures. That is, they are useful until we find our way to the greater visible unity Christ desires for his church. Like congregations, denominations must be humble servants rather than arrogant and autonomous institutions. But properly understood, supported, and held accountable, they are useful members of the body of Christ.

I find joy in our ethos, in the way we Disciples "do" church. We certainly have our limitations and our blind spots, like every denominational family. But being a part of this communion has been an important anchor for millions of Christians through the nineteenth and twentieth centuries. I believe we are a church of the twenty-first century as well.

Questions for Reflection and Discussion

1. What involvement have you personally had in the life of the Disciples of Christ beyond your congregation (e.g., attending an area, regional, or general assembly; attending a racial/ethnic meeting such as the National Convocation; serving on a commission; serving as a camp counselor, etc.)? How did your involvement affect the way you understand "church"?

2. How would you describe our Disciples' ethos? If you were once a part of another communion, how would you describe its ethos?

3. How would you describe the ethos of your own congregation?

4. Can you identify a time or times in your life when accountability to the rest of the denomination helped your congregation to be more faithful and healthy?
5. How would you respond to the question, Why bother with being part of a denomination?

APPENDIX 2

How Is This Body Joined?

We must grow up in every way into him who is the head, into Christ, from whom the whole body, joined and knit together by every ligament with which it is equipped, as each part is working properly, promotes the body's growth in building itself up in love.

Ephesians 4:15–16

In order to begin to think and discern together what God is calling us to be and to do as Disciples of Christ in the years ahead, we need a common understanding of how this communion, this part of the body of Christ, is "joined and knit together."

In all the 2,000 years of church history, there have been three basic ways in which the various communions within the church of Jesus Christ have organized themselves. These three "polities" (forms of church government) are still with us today. They are the *episcopal,* the *presbyterian,* and the *congregational.*

The first of these three forms of church government, the *episcopal,* is the most widely found in all of Christendom. The Roman Catholic Church, the Orthodox churches, the Methodist churches, the Church of England and, yes, the Episcopal Church all have this form of polity. The English word "episcopal" comes from the Greek word, *episcope,* which translates as "oversight." Episcopal polity includes *bishops* who give oversight to the life of the church. The bishops teach and defend the faith. It is important to note that bishops do not generally have the power to define the faith by themselves. The faith is defined by church

155

councils called for that very purpose. The bishops, then, defend the faith as it has been defined by the councils of a particular communion.[1]

The second form of church government, the *presbyterian*, is that which is used by most of the Protestant communions that trace their origins to the sixteenth-century reformer John Calvin. This includes the various Presbyterian and Reform Churches such as the Presbyterian Church in the U.S.A. and the Reform Church of America. "Presbyterian" comes from the Greek word *presbuterion,* which translates as "council of elders." The presbyterian system of government is a representative system. The chief representative body (which is called the "general assembly" in the Presbyterian Church U.S.A.,[2] for example) determines answers to questions about the nature of the faith and decides how the denomination as a whole stands on various issues. Locally, presbyteries (bodies composed of locally elected representatives) are responsible for the accountability of ministers and members in matters of faith and practice.

The third form of church government is called *congregational,* and it is the form of polity that is used, for example, by the Baptist conventions and by the Christian Church (Disciples of Christ). In these churches, each congregation makes its own decisions in regard to who its minister shall be, what shall happen to its property, what its budget and program will be, and what its position on various issues will be. Within this congregational polity, individuals generally have the freedom to decide for themselves matters of faith and individual practice. Thus, even when a communion with a congregational form of polity comes together in an assembly or convention, the decisions made by that body in regard to matters of conscience are not binding on the individual congregation or individual members themselves.

Each of these three forms of polity are found in rudimentary form in the New Testament. A biblical example of the episcopal form can be found in Paul, who acted much like a bishop, visiting

---

[1] In most episcopal communions, the composition of such councils generally includes the bishops but includes other officers or representatives (ordained and lay) of the church as well.
[2] Although our Disciples general church meeting is also called a General Assembly, ours has a different composition and a different role in our church's life.

and writing congregations, defending the faith against the encroachment of non-Christian ideas and practices (e.g., Gal. 1:6f). An example of the presbyterian form can be found in the Council of Jerusalem, which was a group of apostles and elders who met to consider whether Gentiles had to be circumcised in order to become Christians (Acts 15:1f). An example of the congregational form can be found in the congregation in Corinth deciding how much it would contribute to an offering for the wider church (2 Cor. 9:1–5, RSV). Each form of polity has its advantages and disadvantages.

Because the Christian Church (Disciples of Christ) has a congregational polity, let's look a bit more closely at this form of governance. Within congregational communions there are differences of degree. Some groups are *radically* congregational. These groups, including, for example, the Churches of Christ, which grew out of the Stone-Campbell tradition (not to be confused with the *United* Church of Christ), have almost no organizational life or structures beyond the congregation. The independence and autonomy[3] of each congregation is strongly guarded. The Independent Christian Churches, also having grown out of the Stone-Campbell tradition, have somewhat more structure, including a North American Convention, but nevertheless reject the notion of a centralized organization to qualify, send, and support overseas missionaries, for example.

The Disciples of Christ were also rather radically congregational until 1968, when we restructured ourselves. By this action we went from being a kind of association of autonomous congregations, schools, agencies, and missionary societies into a new kind of structure that recognizes that all of us Disciples together are part of *one* church. We changed our name accordingly from The International Convention of the Christian Church*es* (Disciples of Christ) to the Christian Church (Disciples of Christ). So, beginning in 1968, we have developed a kind of *modified* congregationalism, which can be called a *covenantal polity.* Our Statement of Identity reflects this covenantal polity when it says, "The Christian Church (Disciples of Christ) is a

---

[3]A word that never appears in the New Testament. Its literal meaning is "a law unto itself," which is certainly not a biblical concept of church.

community of believers who through baptism into Jesus Christ are bound by covenant to God and to one another."

The Nature of Our Covenant as Disciples of Christ

A covenant is a solemn promise that binds two or more parties together in specific ways. In English, the word "testament" means a *covenant* between parties. One's "last will and testament," for example, is a covenant between an individual and the state as to how his or her estate shall be distributed at the time of death. Thus, the Old Testament is the story of the original covenant between God and Israel and the New Testament is the story of the new covenant between God and the church of Jesus Christ.

In the Old Testament, it is clear that Israel understood itself to be related to God through a covenant that was initiated by God. In Leviticus 26:12, God says, "I…will be your God, and you shall be my people," and the terms of this covenant are laid out: what God will do and what Israel must do in order to remain faithful to the covenant. Israel's primary responsibility in the relationship was to obey the law of God, especially the Ten Commandments. The prophets proclaimed God's faithfulness to the covenant and continually called Israel to return to faithfulness in the face of their frequent *un*faithfulness. Jeremiah longed for the day when the covenant would no longer need to be enforced by the law but would be written upon the hearts of people.

In the New Testament, it is clear that the early church regarded themselves as bound to God and to one another in a covenantal relationship. Like Israel, they had been "made a people" by God and had been *called* into the body of Christ; they were the *ekklesia* (a Greek word meaning "community of the called"). They experienced joy in this new covenant and celebrated it in their central act of worship, the Lord's supper. This holy meal included the drinking of wine, which was understood as the sacramental symbol of the blood of Jesus, which was shed to seal this new covenant.[4] This new covenant was no longer enforced by the law but was, as Jeremiah had hoped, written on the hearts of the followers of Christ.

---

[4]"This cup is the new covenant in my blood. Do this, as often as you drink it, in remembrance of me" (1 Cor. 11:25).

The covenant that is at the heart of the Christian Church (Disciples of Christ) is rooted in this same new covenant that has always been the foundation of the church of Jesus Christ. It is a three-way covenant between God, us, and one another. We understand ourselves to be part of the *ekklesia,* the community of the called. We live not by a contract that emphasizes *rights*, but by a covenant that emphasizes *responsibilities*. A *contractual* way of life invites "winner take all" strategies and the competitive hoarding of the church's gifts. A *covenantal* way of life together, however, calls for interdependence, synergy, and the sharing of resources. It also calls for mutual accountability to one another before God.

Maturing from Individualism to Covenant

As it developed in the early 1800s, the Stone-Campbell movement was described in many ways, including "an experiment in liberty." It was a time when there was a tyranny of denominational structures from which the individual needed rescue. Like most Americans, Disciples *reveled* in individualism, and since, culturally speaking, this was like "swimming downstream," we grew like wildfire across the frontier; however, we soon began to see the limits of radical individualism and began seeking cooperative approaches to ministry and mission. In the mid-nineteenth century, rudimentary forms such as the antecedents of regions and the American Christian Missionary Society began taking shape as ways of fostering cooperative work among Disciples.

If there is anything we have learned, or should have learned, from our experiment in liberty, it is the importance of connection and relationship. In fact, our restructure in 1968 was an effort to give form to a new covenantal polity that offered "connectedness" within a context of responsible individual freedom.

Today we face a radically different cultural context in our church life than that which we were experiencing in 1968. The individualism of our North American culture, which Americans and Canadians have mostly enjoyed and celebrated, is now being lived out in a context in which value systems and institutions have broken down. We have reached a point where individuals make moral judgments almost entirely on the basis of their internal feelings and perceptions, without serious reference to external ethical perspectives (including those of the church).

Duane Cummins, a Disciples church historian, has described our new reality this way: "In the nineteenth century, it was the individual who needed protection from the tyranny of the church. In the twentieth century, it is the church that needs protection from the tyranny of the individual."[5] So we continue our struggle to find a way of relating the parts and pieces of this church in a way that is freeing yet responsible. Mere denominational structures beyond the congregation cannot accomplish this alone, and if anyone tries to *impose* an order on this church through regional and general structures, we will simply recreate the tyranny of structures from which we rebelled originally, and we will experience new rebellions. The regional and general manifestations have been authorized to do a number of ministries on behalf of the whole church and have even been authorized to provide significant means of accountability (especially for the ministry). But we must never forget that we are a covenantal body in which all of us as individuals and as congregations, regional and general units, and other institutions and organizations within the body *have volunteered* to be a part of the whole, to be in covenant with one another and with God.

We Disciples are yet on a pilgrimage, and we need to maintain flexibility in our structures. Our life will be marked by continual change and the need for flexibility, just as people on a pilgrimage pitch their tent now here and now there as they move down the road. As Cummins put it, *The Design* gave us the possibility of "more equitable balance between some of our ageless polarities: freedom and community, unity and diversity, congregationalism and catholicity."[6]

Nevertheless, the human condition is such that structures have a tendency to demand service rather than remaining servants. Thus, we must always remember that the primary

[5]Duane Cummins, from an address to the Nebraska Regional Assembly in November, 1998: "Alexander Campbell: Messenger of Reform."
[6]Duane Cummins, *A Handbook for Today's Disciples*, rev. ed. (St. Louis: Chalice Press, 1991), p. 11.

purpose of the regional and general manifestations is not to be ends in themselves, but to enhance the faithfulness and effectiveness of congregations, providing ways and means for congregations to address the world faithfully and effectively.

With the separation of the Churches of Christ in the late 1800s, we Disciples said no to radical restorationism. With the separation of the Independent congregations, we said no to radical congregational autonomy. So to what did we say yes? We said yes to covenantal relationship, which is made real through a covenantal form of church government, a covenantal polity.

The challenge of the nineteenth century was the frontier, where religious sectarianism was rampant. The challenge of the twentieth century was the city, where secularism was rampant. The challenge of the twenty-first century is the parochialism by which people define reality and community in narrower and narrower terms. With its balance of freedom and responsibility, individualism and corporate accountability, our covenantal polity is ideal for this kind of day.

Living in covenant means general and regional church life must be lived in *serious* reference to congregational life and to individual members' perceptions of what the wider church is doing on their behalf. At the same time, covenantal polity means that congregations and individual Disciples must take the wider church seriously and not live in splendid isolation, oblivious to the rest of the body.

The great challenge now, therefore, is to connect people across the great schisms of the day, across the lines of social and political and theological balkanization that are so prominent in North American life generally and in church life specifically.

Thus, to be in covenant means, in part, that congregations, regions, general units, and other institutions of the church all give up some of their autonomy in order to accomplish common aims and purposes for the sake of the gospel of Jesus Christ. Before 1968, for example, persons were ordained to Disciples ministry by congregations acting on their own. But after 1968, congregations began sharing with regions the responsibility of deciding who should or should not be ordained. Thus, today, when a person wishes to be ordained, he or she must be approved by a congregation *and* by the region of which that congregation is a part. This change in procedure has been helpful in ensuring greater accountability on the part of ministers and congregations to the Disciples ethos and to the whole communion.

In a radically congregational system, congregations are seen as the only "real" expression of church beyond individual Christians. Thus, any forms of organization beyond the congregation (mission boards, mission societies, etc.) are regarded as being only agencies or instruments of the churches (i.e., the congregations). But in our Disciples modified congregationalism with our covenantal polity, such structures beyond the congregation are also understood to be truly church. In fact, we speak of the one church manifesting itself in three ways: congregationally, regionally (areas and districts are parts of regions), and generally. This is often referred to as three manifestations of church: the congregational, regional, and general. It is important to note here that the congregational, regional, and general manifestations are not each "churches" in or by themselves. Rather, they are three manifestations of the *one* church called the Christian Church (Disciples of Christ). Each of these manifestations is fully church only when it stands in covenantal relationship with the other two. Any one of these three manifestations is incomplete and not fully church apart from the other two.

So when we are meeting in a congregational meeting, we are church. When we meet in regional assembly, we are church. When we are doing mission work in, say, the nation of Lesotho in southern Africa through the Division of Overseas Ministries, we are church. Yet, in each case, we are only part of the whole Christian Church (Disciples of Christ).

Perhaps these seem to some to be unimportant distinctions or even just semantics, but these concepts are at the very heart of how we work and live as the Christian Church (Disciples of Christ). These concepts reside at the very heart of what it means to be in covenant with one another under the sovereignty of Jesus Christ.

We Disciples are a people of the table—the communion table. The table, rather than a body of doctrine, is at the center of our life together, reminding us that we are part of the body by the grace of God and that we are called to live grace-fully with each other. Thus, when we are at our best, our congregational, regional, and general life is an expression of covenant, as we care for one another even in the face of our differences of opinion.

Each of the three kinds of church polities (episcopal, presbyterian, and congregational) and their variations have strengths and weaknesses. The rudiments of each of these polities can be found in the New Testament, and elements of all three can be found in our Disciples polity. Speaking for myself, while I appreciate the strengths of the other systems (and there are certainly those days when I wish we had one of the other two forms of polity!), I appreciate the strengths of our modified congregationalism, our *covenantal polity*, and I am committed to making it an effective and faithful expression of the church God wills even as I seek to work with the weaknesses.

We are *in covenant*, meaning we are ethically and spiritually bound to cooperate with one another because, having accepted God's covenant with us, we have entered into this covenantal polity with one another *and with God.* So while we are not legally bound to work together, neither is working together optional: It is the essence of the church. Our strength comes from the fact that we work together because we are called to faithfulness, not because we are legally bound to do so.

When we are at our best, we discover that God has granted us just the right balance of freedom and responsibility. This is how this church works. When it does not work, it is usually because someone embraced the freedom of the covenant but forsook the implied responsibility to work together as the whole community of Christ's church.

I believe our covenantal polity is a faithful expression of the church God wills. In fact, I believe this is the polity of the future for most of the church of Jesus Christ. I believe I already see the polities of many other communions moving in the direction of covenantal polity. Nevertheless, we Disciples have a great deal of maturing to do if we are to claim that we truly live by a covenantal polity. We need to spend more time reflecting on who God is calling us to be and seeking to understand what the implications of that are for what we do and how we do it.

Questions for Reflection and Discussion

1. Name three advantages and three disadvantages of each of the three basic polities (episcopal, presbyterian, and congregational).
2. In what ways has your congregation used the services offered through your region in recent years? (Name as many as you can.)
3. In what ways has your congregation used the services offered through general units in recent years? (Name as many as you can.)
4. How much does your congregation contribute annually to Basic Mission Finance? (Be sure to include gifts made by the women's, men's, and youth fellowships as well as special day offerings.) What percentage of your congregation's total offerings does this represent? (This information can be gleaned from the annual *Yearbook of the Christian Church (Disciples of Christ),* of which your congregation's office or library probably has a copy. Your regional church office can also provide this information.)
5. In what ways could you *personally* contribute toward making our covenantal polity work?